NATURE AQUARIUM
WORLD

by Takashi Amano

All photos taken by the author.

PREFACE: A MODEL OF NATURE

Every other year for the past twenty years or so I've gone to a university in Niigata to give a lecture. Every time I decide it will be my last, but then I always accept the next invitation. Without a doubt I go for the Agano River, the delicious fishes of the Sea of Japan, and a certain quiet onsen (hot spring) I visit after the lecture.

For the past ten years, however, there has been another reason for making the trip—going to see Takashi Amano's aquaria. There is usually quite a crowd there: Mr. and Mrs. Nagashima, Mr. and Mrs. Iizuka, Mr. and Mrs. Ogawa, Takashi's older brother, and several others. To understand how wonderful his aquaria are, one just has to read this book. But even this book can do them only slight justice.

I think the first time he let me see them was on February 2, 1982. I thought the fishes were just wonderful, but the fantastic plants left me flabbergasted. There was something so attractive about them, though, and every time they were different. It wasn't like some disappointing exhibition that was concerned only with volume. It's hard to describe, but they made me feel a kind of stability, a peacefulness.

Ecosystem exhibits have become popular at public aquariums. If the subject is fishes, they build a little habitat that looks like where the fishes live. Too often, I feel, they are a poor representation of nature, a stilted miniature like a bonsai. It seems that the more people try to shut nature up in an aquarium, or try to capture nature itself, the more twisted that "nature" becomes.

Takashi hasn't told me so himself, but his aquaria are clearly the opposite of that. One doesn't find this kind of nature everywhere. And so I think his aquaria truly are models of nature. As a researcher of lake and stream ecology, I want to express my admiration for the power and peacefulness of these aquaria.

Dr. Kawanabe, Professor of Science, Kyoto University, and Director of the Ecology Research Center, January 5, 1992

TRANSLATED BY CHRISTOPER PERRIUS

1996 Edition

Distributed in the UNITED STATES to the Pet Trade by T.F.H. Publications, Inc., One T.F.H. Plaza, Neptune City, NJ 07753; distributed in the UNITED STATES to the Bookstore and Library Trade by National Book Network, Inc. 4720 Boston Way, Lanham MD 20706; in CANADA to the Pet Trade by H & L Pet Supplies Inc., 27 Kingston Crescent, Kitchener, Ontario N2B 2T6; Rolf C. Hagen Inc., 3225 Sartelon St. Laurent-Montreal Quebec H4R 1E8; in CANADA to the Book Trade by Vanwell Publishing Ltd., 1 Northrup Crescent, St. Catharines, Ontario L2M 6P5 ; in ENGLAND by T.F.H. Publications, PO Box 15, Waterlooville PO7 6BQ; in AUSTRALIA AND THE SOUTH PACIFIC by T.F.H. (Australia), Pty. Ltd., Box 149, Brookvale 2100 N.S.W., Australia; in NEW ZEALAND by Brooklands Aquarium Ltd. 5 McGiven Drive, New Plymouth, RD1 New Zealand; in Japan by T.F.H. Publications, Japan—Jiro Tsuda, 10-12-3 Ohjidai, Sakura, Chiba 285, Japan; in SOUTH AFRICA by Lopis (Pty) Ltd., P.O. Box 39127, Booysens, 2016, Johannesburg, South Africa. Published by T.F.H. Publications, Inc.

BY T.F.H. PUBLICATIONS, INC.

NATURE AQUARIUM
WORLD

PROLOGUE

who can ever grow tired of the sight of brightly colored fishes swimming among flourishing underwater plants? Memories of playing in rivers and ponds as a child well up inside, or you just get lost in the amazing world that unfolds before you. Though people aspire to make a copy or imitation of nature when they build an aquarium, it's really an impossible task. The aquarium is a unique combination of two kinds of creativity: human and natural. It can be thought of as a glass crucible where these two creative energies mix and mingle. The results? Fascination and relaxation.

CONTENTS

PUBLISHER'S NOTES

This book was originally published by Marine Planning Company of Tokyo, Japan under the title *NATURE AQUARIUM WORLD*. We discovered this book in EVERY tropical fish store we visited in Japan. Each dealer used the book as his personal reference and in each store we found at least one nature world aquarium. The term *nature world* seems an odd one for English-speaking people. But when you analyze the book you realize that the term truly identifies the book.

The author, Takashi Amano, is a portrait painter who uses an aquarium as his canvas and aquatic plants as his paints. His scenes are taken from nature. He copies nature as it exists in his eyes. He traveled the world to capture the scenes in magnificent photographs and then he transformed them into planted aquariums which are his rendering. These renderings can only be described as nature world aquariums. Is there a more fitting name for them?

Having read and edited just about every aquarium and aquarium plant book in existence, I can safely say that this is the most thrilling and exciting book on the subject I have ever read. I hope you enjoy it too.

Prof. Dr. Herbert R. Axelrod
May, 1994
Neptune, New Jersey

QUARIUM

A LITTLE PARK

This layout is centered around a leaning vertical rock and a
horizontal rock, a common arrangement in Zen gardening.
The well-trimmed pearl grass lends depth to the construction.
Designed in the spirit of a Zen garden, this layout comfortably
fits a lot of life into a limited space.

NO. 1 DATA

■ PHOTOGRAPHING : DECEMBER 1991
■ WATER TANK : W315XD300XH244 (mm)
■ CONTENT : 12 liters
■ MAINTENANCE
● LIGHTING : 30W (WITH FAN)
● FILTERING : OUTSIDE, HANGING FILTER
● SUBSTRATE : SEA SAND
● CO_2 SUPPLY : ONCE EVERY FIVE SECONDS
● FERTILIZATION : 0.16cc/liter
● WATER CHANGE : ONCE A WEEK, 1/2 TANK OF WATER
■ WATER CONDITION
● TEMPERATURE : 26°C
● pH VALUE : 6.8
● TOTAL HARDNESS (GH) : 2°dH
● CARBONATE HARDNESS (KH) : 2°dH
● NITRITE (NO_2) : LESS THAN 0.1mg/liter
● NITRATE (NO_3) : LESS THAN 10mg/liter
● CO_2 : 16mg/liter
● O_2 : 7mg/liter

WATERSCAPE WITH ROCK

Also influenced by Zen gardens, this design makes
good use of foreground space. It is constructed from a
standing rock and several different-sized horizontal
rocks. The normally delicate *Rotala wallichii* seems to

KILLIFISH FOREST

A fine balance is attained between lush green grass in the background and the *Glossostigma* and trimmed pearl grass in the foreground, while the bright *Riccia* running through the center adds sparkle.

NO. 3 DATA

- ■ PHOTOGRAPHING : DECEMBER 1991
- ■ WATER TANK : W398XD254XH280(mm)
- ■ CONTENT : 23 liters
- ■ MAINTENANCE
- ● LIGHTING : 40W (WITH FAN)
- ● FILTERING : OUTSIDE, HANGING FILTER
- ● SUBSTRATE : SEA SAND
- ● CO_2 SUPPLY : ONCE EVERY FIVE SECONDS
- ● FERTILIZATION : 0.2cc/liters
- ● WATER CHANGE : ONCE A WEEK, 1/2 TANK OF WATER
- ■ WATER CONDITION
- ● TEMPERATURE : 24°C
- ● pH VALUE : 6.9
- ● TOTAL HARDNESS (GH) : 3°dH
- ● CARBONATE HARDNESS (KH) : 3°dH
- ● NITRITE (NO_2) : LESS THAN 0.1mg/liter
- ● NITRATE (NO_3) : LESS THAN 10mg/liter
- ● CO_2 : 15mg/liter
- ● O_2 : 7mg/liter

GORGEOUS GUPPIES

This waterscape uses only bright plants in a simple
triangular design. The dynamism of the composition
makes the work appear larger than the tank that
houses it. The guppies move like flamenco dancers
across a stage of green.

NO. 4 DATA

- ■ PHOTOGRAPHING : DECEMBER 1991
- ■ WATER TANK : W450XD295XH300(mm)
- ■ CONTENT : 35 liters
- ■ MAINTENANCE
- ● LIGHTING : 60W
- ● FILTERING : OUTSIDE, HANGING FILTER
- ● SUBSTRATE : SEA SAND
- ● CO_2 SUPPLY : ONCE EVERY FIVE SECONDS
- ● FERTILIZATION : 0.2cc/liters
- ● WATER CHANGE : ONCE A WEEK, 1/2 TANK OF WATER
- ■ WATER CONDITION
- ● TEMPERATURE : 25°C
- ● pH VALUE : 7.0
- ● TOTAL HARDNESS (GH) : 3°dH
- ● CARBONATE HARDNESS (KH) : 3°dH
- ● NITRITE (NO_2) : LESS THAN 0.1mg/liter
- ● NITRATE (NO_3) : LESS THAN 10mg/liter
- ● CO_2 : 14mg/liter
- ● O_2 : 7mg/liter

NATURE AT ARM'S LENGTH

A certain American psychiatrist recommends watching guppies as a therapy for depression. Rather than taking some kind of medicine, the sight of the small yet vital guppy should pull the patient out of his or her dark shell.

Not just depression and hypertension, but ulcers and all stress-related disorders that arise from the complexity of our lives are on the increase, even, most disturbingly, among grammar school children. When I see the damage these pressures cause, I cannot help but lose confidence in the social system.

Japan has become a great economic power, and a country where we have cultural freedom. We have come to want the good things in life, and we don't waste our time with low-quality products. We certainly are much richer economically than our ancestors in the Edo Era, but how about spiritually?

Though surrounded by unsullied nature, the pet industry boomed in the Edo days, with much success gained in breeding quality dogs, birds, and goldfish. The Meiji writer Koizumi was impressed by the Edo merchants who built thriving businesses by specializing in sales of grasshoppers and crickets. That age's love of small creatures is impressive.

With this kind of past, Japanese people should have a special feeling for living in and with nature. As environmental destruction continues, I believe that more and more people will instinctively realize the need for coexistence with the natural world and will also want to have a bit of nature within arm's length.

Many Japanese my age got their first impression of Africa from comic books with titles like *Jungle Empire,* and many people still imagine it as the "dark" continent. But when I went to visit there, I realized that "colorful" continent might be a better name for Africa. Nairobi, the capital of Kenya, is a

A DISTANT PLAIN

A plain where a fresh wind sways the spring grasses–this arrangement achieves a depth and breadth that create an image of a plain of green stretching as far as the eye can see.

NO. 5 DATA

- ■ PHOTOGRAPHING : MAY 1991
- ■ WATER TANK : W600XD300XH360(mm)
- ■ CONTENT : 56 liters
- ■ MAINTENANCE
- ● LIGHTING : 20W X 3(60W)
- ● FILTERING : POWER FILTER
- ● SUBSTRATE : AKADAMA CERAMICS
- ● CO_2 SUPPLY : ONCE EVERY FIVE SECONDS
- ● FERTILIZATION : 0.1cc/liters
- ● WATER CHANGE : ONCE A WEEK, 1/2 TANK OF WATER
- ■ WATER CONDITION
- ● TEMPERATURE : 26°C
- ● pH VALUE : 6.9
- ● TOTAL HARDNESS (GH) : 2°dH
- ● CARBONATE HARDNESS (KH) : 2°dH
- ● NITRITE (NO_2) : LESS THAN 0.1mg/liter
- ● NITRATE (NO_3) : LESS THAN 10mg/liter
- ● CO_2 : 15mg/liter
- ● O_2 : 7mg/liter

beautiful city of flowers and tree-lined boulevards. Street corners and trash bins are surrounded with rainbows of flowers. I've never seen such beautiful garbage cans! There is less littering, because people want to be near the trash bins. There is a psychological factor at work here.

Just outside the city is the Nairobi Zoo, where wild animals such as lions, giraffes, and zebras are kept. Several years before, someone was killed by a lion that they were trying to videotape less than a kilometer from the city center. I was amazed by how much the people of Kenya value their wildlife. It is not unusual for a herd of giraffes or elephants to cross the road suddenly, but drivers never sound the horn or try to inch their way through. No matter how many animals there are, the drivers invariably rest their knee upon the steering wheel, sit back, and wait. This amusing sight is encountered on any long trip in Kenya. Well, that's the way it was in 1974 when I first visited, and herds of animals were seen everywhere...

When I returned to Japan I took the train from the airport to Ueno Station, one of Tokyo's largest. I saw people pushing each other out of the way to save a few seconds, shoving for prime spots on the train. I couldn't detect a shred of the spirit of compromise. When I met spear-toting Masai in Kenya I hadn't felt any fear, but the city dwellers of my home country were truly terrifying.

A ZEN GARDEN

This waterscape attains one of the main goals of Zen Buddhist gardening: to create a great space in a small area. The V-shaped piece of driftwood anchors the composition, and the 17 rocks are arranged in Zen style.

THE DEATH OF A POND

In the spring of 1983, I took a camera around the base of Tsunoda Mountain to see the early spring flowers bloom as the last snow melted. I headed for a nearby pond to see the cherry trees and was greeted by a strong, fishy smell. Near the banks I saw several dead

GATHERING PLACES

This work is reminiscent of a dense jungle. Using a variety of plants, both long– and short–stemmed, and of different colors and shapes, gives the composition a strong sense of perspective.

NO. 7 DATA

- ■ PHOTOGRAPHING : DECEMBER 1990
- ■ WATER TANK : W600XD300XH360(mm)
- ■ CONTENT : 56 liters
- ■ MAINTENANCE
- ● LIGHTING : 20WX3(60W)
- ● FILTERING : POWER FILTER
- ● SUBSTRATE : AKADAMA CERAMICS
- ● CO_2 SUPPLY : ONCE EVERY FIVE SECONDS
- ● FERTILIZATION : 0.1cc/liters
- ● WATER CHANGE : ONCE A WEEK, 1/2 TANK OF WATER
- ■ WATER CONDITION
- ● TEMPERATURE : 27°C
- ● pH VALUE : 7.0
- ● TOTAL HARDNESS (GH) : 3°dH
- ● CARBONATE HARDNESS (KH) : 2°dH
- ● NITRITE (NO_2) : LESS THAN 0.1mg/liter
- ● NITRATE (NO_3) : LESS THAN 10mg/liter
- ● CO_2 : 16mg/liter
- ● O_2 : 8mg/liter

crucian carp floating belly-up and rotten, and the pond water was foamy and without its usual clarity. What had happened?

I hadn't visited the pond in many years but as a child I often went there on field trips. We used to rent boats and play out on the water. Through the clear water we could see Oikawa *(Zacco platypus)* and dace threading their way through the forest of underwater plants. Above them dragonflies buzzed and beetles swam–it was a paradise for fish, fowl, and frog. When had it changed?

I immediately went to ask the curator of the local museum, since I knew his home was near the pond. However, he was surprised and upset by what I told him, and had no idea what had happened. After much investigation, we learned at the city offices that thousands of carp were being released into the pond every year in an attempt to make it a tourist fishing Mecca. This was understandable. The problem was that the fishing lines were getting caught in the yellow pond lilies and water lilies, so they removed these hindrances from the pond by both pulling them out and releasing grass carp (= *Ctenopharyngodon idelus)* to eat them. The pond was turned to sludge by human ignorance and selfishness, and this saddened and angered me.

I explained to the town officials what had killed the pond. It has no spring or stream sources, so it needs plant life like the lotus and water lily to purify the water. Uprooting these plants leads to the death of the pond. The paste bait used by the carp fishermen was extremely rich in nutrients, and when a pond has little

or no purification ability, it will quickly become over-saturated with nutrients and the ecological balance will be destroyed. Since the fishermen were prohibited from keeping what they caught, the fish population of the pond eventually exceeded its natural limits. Finally, the mouth wounds caused by the fishhooks led to an epidemic of mouth fungus, causing further carp attrition. Any one of these factors alone could have led to the destruction of the pond ecosystem, as any aquarist would know.

The town officials decided to fix up the pond. They drained the water and removed the profuse sludge from the bottom as well as the fattened grass carp. Even if it couldn't return completely to the glorious state of the old days, a decent recovery seemed not far off. Water ecosystems are more sensitive than forest ecosystems. However, the following year I saw an article with photos in the local paper headlined "3000 Carp Released into Fishing Pond" I was just dumbfounded.

A LYRICAL WATERSCAPE

When designing this waterscape, I thought of a stream where I used to play in my childhood, and sang a children's song, "Spring Stream" while working on it. It is meant to evoke an idyllic childhood memory of playing in water.

NO. 8 DATA

■ PHOTOGRAPHING : DECEMBER 1991
■ WATER TANK : W600XD300XH360(mm)
■ CONTENT : 56 liters
■ MAINTENANCE
● LIGHTING : 20W X 4(80W)
● FILTERING : POWER FILTER
● SUBSTRATE : OISO SAND
● CO_2 SUPPLY : ONCE EVERY FIVE SECONDS
● FERTILIZATION : 0.1cc/liters
● WATER CHANGE ONCE A WEEK, 1/2 TANK OF WATER
■ WATER CONDITION
● TEMPERATURE : 27°C
● pH VALUE : 6.9
● TOTAL HARDNESS (GH) : 2°dH
● CARBONATE HARDNESS (KH) : 2°dH
● NITRITE (NO_2) : LESS THAN 0.1mg/liter
● NITRATE (NO_3) : LESS THAN 10mg/liter
● CO_2 : 15mg/liter

WATER PLANTS IN GOOD ORDER

The beauty of the streamlined *Hottonia* is emphasized in this work. This is an example of a layout where I had to choose plants that would help me highlight another specific plant.

NO. 9 DATA

- ■ PHOTOGRAPHING . JUNE 1991
- ■ WATER TANK : W600XD300XH360(mm)
- ■ CONTENT : 56 liters
- ■ MAINTENANCE
- ● LIGHTING : 20WX3(60W)
- ● FILTERING : POWER FILTER
- ● SUBSTRATE : AKADAMA CERAMICS
- ● CO_2 SUPPLY : ONCE EVERY FIVE SECONDS
- ● FERTILIZATION : A DROP OF FERTILIZER, EVERDAY

A CORNER OF THE GRASS PATCH

I wanted to recreate the little patches of grass that we see every day yet fail to notice, and which despite their smallness are full of life.

NO. 10 DATA

- ■ PHOTOGRAPHING : OCTOBER 1990
- ■ WATER TANK : W600XD300XH360(mm)
- ■ CONTENT : 56 liters
- ■ MAINTENANCE
- ● LIGHTING : 20WX3(60W)
- ● FILTERING : POWER FILTER
- ● SUBSTRATE : OISO SAND
- ● CO_2 SUPPLY : ONCE EVERY FIVE SECONDS
- ● FERTILIZATION : 0.1cc/liters

AN ENVIRONMENT THAT IS GOOD FOR THE SOUL

When it comes to landscape painting, I'm one of those no-talent enthusiasts. I pretty much stick to photography now, but when I paint I prefer lightly-colored paintings of thatched-roof houses in the mountains or boathouses and fishing villages by the rough Sea of Japan. However, the subjects of these motifs are hard to find these days, and when I do come across such old homes the gardens are unkempt or they have modern sliding-glass doors on them.

When I first visited Africa fifteen years ago, even the lodges and pensions for tourists blended right in with the traditional housing surrounding them. And on a certain Mediterranean island an ordinance requires people to repaint their homes white every year. These kinds of rules are found in many countries, and I admire the people of advanced culture who make them.

I've realized something in my travels, and it may be my own prejudice so I'll state it briefly: people who live in simple, beautiful surroundings are simple and beautiful inside. But as development progresses, the soul is ravaged along with the landscape. So I think that we should make our daily surroundings beautiful. How about requiring every home to have at least one large tree? Every home would have to have the necessary space, and different towns could require different trees: this town apricot, that one zelkova, another ginkgo, and so on. Ugly homes and billboards would be covered up, and eventually neighborhoods would be blanketed in green.

Likewise, aquarists should add some plants every time the fish population increases. Of course the quantity depends on the fishes' size, but a small characin, for example, would require only a few stemmed plants such as *Hygrophila* or *Rotala* to take care of the water purification. Plants and animals balance each other, and this balance needs to be maintained even in the smallest systems.

COMPETING AQUATIC PLANTS

Nature expresses itself to us in many ways. This somewhat surreal waterscape finely balances many contrasting colors.

NO. 11 DATA

- ■ PHOTOGRAPHING : MARCH 1991
- ■ WATER TANK : W600XD300XH360(mm)
- ■ CONTENT : 56 liters
- ■ MAINTENANCE
- ● LIGHTING : 20W X 3(60W)
- ● FILTERING : POWER FILTER
- ● SUBSTRATE : AKADAMA CERAMICS
- ● CO_2 SUPPLY : ONCE EVERY FIVE SECONDS
- ● FERTILIZATION : 0.1cc/liters
- ● WATER CHANGE : ONCE A WEEK, 1/2 TANK OF WATER
- ■ WATER CONDITION
- ● TEMPERATURE : 26°C
- ● pH VALUE : 6.9
- ● TOTAL HARDNESS (GH) : 2°dH
- ● CARBONATE HARDNESS (KH) : 3°dH
- ● NITRITE (NO_2) : 0.1mg/liter
- ● NITRATE (NO_3) : LESS THAN 10mg/liter
- ● CO_2 : 18mg/liter
- ● O_2 : 7mg/liter

AFTER A JAPANESE GARDEN

This layout reproduces the style of a Japanese garden in a 60cm tank. This design eschews the formal or stylistic beauty of the flower bed for the natural beauty of wabi-sabi, the Japanese sense of quiet refinement tinged with the sadness of transience.

NO. 12 DATA

- ■ PHOTOGRAPHING : APRIL 1991
- ■ WATER TANK : W600XD300XH360(mm)
- ■ CONTENT : 56 liters
- ■ MAINTENANCE
- ● LIGHTING : 20WX4(80W)
- ● FILTERING : POWER FILTER
- ● SUBSTRATE : AKADAMA CERAMICS
- ● CO_2 SUPPLY : ONCE EVERY FIVE SECONDS
- ● FERTILIZATION : ONCE EVERY THREE DAYS, A LITTLE
- ● WATER CHANGE : ONCE EVERY TEN DAYS, 1/2 TANK OF WATER
- ■ WATER CONDITION
- ● TEMPERATURE : 25°C
- ● pH VALUE : 6.8
- ● TOTAL HARDNESS (GH) . 2°dH
- ● CARBONATE HARDNESS (KH) . 2°dH
- ● NITRITE (NO_2) : LESS THAN 0.1mg/liter
- ● NITRATE (NO_3) : LESS THAN 10mg/liter
- ● CO_2 : 18mg/liter
- ● O_2 : 7mg/liter

A GLITTERING PLAIN

In the foreground a carpet of *Riccia*, and in the
background hair grass. Beneath bright sunlight the
Riccia is photosynthesizing, and tiny air bubbles
sparkle around the grass.

NO. 13 DATA

- ■ PHOTOGRAPHING : OCTOBER 1991
- ■ WATER TANK : W600XD300XH360(mm)
- ■ CONTENT : 56 liters
- ■ MAINTENANCE
- ● LIGHTING : 20WX4(80W)
- ● FILTERING : POWER FILTER
- ● SUBSTRATE : CERAMICS OF AKADAMA
- ● CO_2 SUPPLY : ONCE EVERY FIVE SECONDS
- ● FERTILIZATION : 0.1cc/liters
- ● WATER CHANGE : ONCE A WEEK, 1/3 TANK OF WATER
- ■ WATER CONDITION
- ● TEMPERATURE : 25°C
- ● pH VALUE : 6.8
- ● TOTAL HARDNESS (GH) : 2°dH
- ● CARBONATE HARDNESS (KH) : 2°dH
- ● NITRITE (NO_2) : LESS THAN 0.1mg/liter
- ● NITRATE (NO_3) : LESS THAN 10mg/liter
- ● CO_2 : 16mg/liter
- ● O_2 : 8mg/liter

MEMORIES OF THE KOREAN PARADISE FISH (CHÔSENBUNA)

I think only older folk are familiar with the Korean Paradise Fish *(Macropodus ocellatus)* because they have been scarce in Japan since the late 1950's. It would be no exaggeration to say that it is nearing

SHINY NEW GREEN

A forest of new green burns with the light of life received from the sun. That mystical shine grabs the observer and doesn't let go.

NO. 14 DATA

- PHOTOGRAPHING : NOVEMBER 1991
- WATER TANK : W600XD300XH360(mm)
- CONTENT : 56 liters
- MAINTENANCE
- LIGHTING : 20W X 4(80W)
- FILTERING : POWER FILTER
- SUBSTRATE : SEA SAND
- CO_2 SUPPLY : ONCE EVERY THREE SECONDS
- FERTILIZATION : 0.2cc/liters
- WATER CHANGE : ONCE A WEEK, 1/3 TANK OF WATER
- WATER CONDITION
- TEMPERATURE : 26°C
- pH VALUE : 6.9
- TOTAL HARDNESS (GH) : 1°dH
- CARBONATE HARDNESS (KH) : 2°dH
- NITRITE (NO_2) : LESS THAN 0.1mg/liter
- NITRATE (NO_3) : LESS THAN 10mg/liter
- CO_2 : 17mg/liter
- O_2 : 8mg/liter

extinction, so I wonder why it hasn't been placed on the endangered species list. The species is not native to Japan but came from the Korean Peninsula, as the name would suggest. The first specimens were brought back to Japan in 1914 by one Akiyama Kichigoro, who was known as the king of Fukugawa goldfish in Tokyo. They escaped from his ornamental pond in the great flood of September 30, 1917 and spread around the Kanto plain. The population exploded in Niigata in the early Showa days (late 1920's), and my friends and I would see practically no other fish in the ponds and rivers where we played. It looked just like its relative, the famous fighting fish from Thailand. When I saw it display its audacious reds and purples in spawning season, I understood why Akiyama had taken the trouble to bring it back.

It had the nasty temper of its cousin and would kill any goldfish kept with it. I loved them, though, and kept some in a small vat with some Mizuwarabi and Tanukimo. It was full of plants like this photo, and the still water was perfect for them. On a spring day I'll never forget, I looked into the vat to see a strange sight that I didn't understand at the time since I was only a young boy: the colorful male and female in an embrace, spawning in a nest made of bubbles.

VIVID REDS

This layout is built around the two types of red water plants. The hard part is striking a balance with such strong colors.

NO. 15 DATA

- ■ PHOTOGRAPHING : JANUARY 1990
- ■ WATER TANK : W600XD300XH450(mm)
- ■ CONTENT : 80 liters
- ■ MAINTENANCE
- ● LIGHTING : 20WX4(80W)
- ● FILTERING : POWER FILTER
- ● SUBSTRATE : OISO SAND
- ● CO_2 SUPPLY : ONCE EVERY FIVE SECONDS
- ● FERTILIZATION : UNNECESSARY
- ● WATER CHANGE : ONCE EVERY TWO WEEKS, 1/2 TANK OF WATER
- ■ WATER CONDITION
- ● TEMPERATURE : 28°C
- ● pH VALUE : 6.5
- ● TOTAL HARDNESS (GH) : 2°dH

GRASSES ON THE WATERSIDE

This waterscape reproduces the changes seen from
bank to river bottom.

NO. 16 DATA

- ■ PHOTOGRAPHING : DECEMBER 1990
- ■ WATER TANK : W600XD300XH450(mm)
- ■ CONTENT : 80 liters
- ■ MAINTENANCE
- ● LIGHTING : 20WX3(60W)
- ● FILTERING : POWER FILTER
- ● SUBSTRATE : OISO SAND
- ● CO_2 SUPPLY : ONCE EVERY FIVE SECONDS
- ● FERTILIZATION : UNNECESSARY
- ● WATER CHANGE : ONCE EVERY TWO WEEKS, 1/2 TANK OF WATER
- ■ WATER CONDITION
- ● TEMPERATURE : 24°C
- ● pH VALUE : 6.5
- ● TOTAL HARDNESS (GH) : 3°dH
- ● CARBONATE HARDNESS (KH) : 3°dH
- ● NITRITE (NO_2) : 0.1mg/liter
- ● NITRATE (NO_3) : LESS THAN 10mg/liter
- ● CO_2 : 15mg/liter
- ● O_2 : 7mg/liter

FLOURISHING CRYPTOS

This work uses only plants that grow wild in Southeast
Asia and resembles a native jungle river where
Rasbora come from. This environment is the most
comfortable for them.

NO. 17 DATA

- ■ PHOTOGRAPHING : NOVEMBER 1990
- ■ WATER TANK : W600XD300XH450(mm)
- ■ CONTENT : 80 liters
- ■ MAINTENANCE
- ● LIGHTING : 20W X 4(80W)
- ● FILTERING : POWER FILTER
- ● SUBSTRATE : OISO SAND
- ● CO_2 SUPPLY : ONCE EVERY FIVE SECONDS
- ● FERTILIZATION : 0.1cc/liters
- ● WATER CHANGE : ONCE A WEEK, 1/3 TANK OF WATER
- ■ WATER CONDITION
- ● TEMPERATURE : 25°C
- ● pH VALUE : 6.8
- ● TOTAL HARDNESS (GH) : 1°dH
- ● CARBONATE HARDNESS (KH) : 1°dH
- ● NITRITE (NO_2) : 0.1mg/liter
- ● NITRATE (NO_3) : LESS THAN 10mg/liter
- ● CO_2 : 16mg/liter
- ● O_2 : 7mg/liter

LAYOUT TIPS

1. Over a base layer of fertilizer, evenly spread thoroughly washed, large granule sand 7-8cm deep in the front and 12-14cm in the back.

2. The finished layout in mind, arrange the driftwood and stones. It's best to decide where the plants will go at this point, too.

3. Since we've decided on a Southeast Asian motif, plant most of the various *Cryptocoryne* spp. in the central area.

4. Between the *Cryptocoryne*, plant the hair grass that will serve as the bottom plant layer.

5. Fill the tank about 70% full and add some long-stemmed plants. Plant tongs are good for this task.

6. After all the planting is done, even out the visible substrate line and any other rough spots.

DYED IN NEW GREEN

This work has a strong spring theme. The open space in the foreground gives it a pastoral feeling, which is supported by the light background colors.

NO. 18 DATA

- PHOTOGRAPHING : DECEMBER 1990
- WATER TANK : W600XD300XH450(mm)
- CONTENT : 80 liters
- MAINTENANCE
  - LIGHTING : 20WX4(80W)
  - FILTERING : POWER FILTER
  - SUBSTRATE : OISO SAND
  - CO_2 SUPPLY : ONCE EVERY FIVE SECONDS

PAINTING THE RIVER BANK

This was my first study of an aquarium based on a Japanese stream, and it uses only plants native to Japan. The driftwood is arranged in the "golden section," the harmonious ratio of two sections (approx. 5:3), and is the pivot on which the composition turns.

NO. 19 DATA

- ■ PHOTOGRAPHING : FEBRUARY1989
- ■ WATER TANK : W600XD450XH450(mm)
- ■ CONTENT : 120 liters
- ■ MAINTENANCE
- ● LIGHTING : 20WX4(80W)
- ● FILTERING : POWER FILTER
- ● SUBSTRATE : OISO SAND
- ● CO_2 SUPPLY : ONCE EVERY FIVE SECONDS, A DROP OF CO_2
- ● FERTILIZATION : UNNECESSARY
- ● WATER CHANGE : ONCE A WEEK, 1/2 TANK OF WATER
- ■ WATER CONDITION
- ● TEMPERATURE : 23°C
- ● pH VALUE : 7.0
- ● TOTAL HARDNESS (GH) : 3°dH
- ● CARBONATE HARDNESS (KH) : 2°dH
- ● NITRITE (NO_2) : 0.1mg/liter
- ● NITRATE (NO_3) : LESS THAN 10mg/liter
- ● CO_2 : 16mg/liter
- ● O_2 : 7mg/liter

WATER PLANT TANSAI

All of the plants used in this aquarium are delicate and light-colored, chosen to imitate the soft and gentle world of tansai painting, a Japanese school that uses light colors.

NO. 20 DATA

- ■ PHOTOGRAPHING : FEBRUARY 1990
- ■ WATER TANK : W600XD450XH450(mm)
- ■ CONTENT : 120 liters
- ■ MAINTENANCE
- ● LIGHTING : 20W X 6(120W)
- ● FILTERING : POWER FILTER(X2)
- ● SUBSTRATE : OISO SAND
- ● CO_2 SUPPLY : ONCE EVERY THREE SECONDS
- ● FERTILIZATION : 0.1cc/liters
- ● WATER CHANGE : ONCE A WEEK, 1/2 TANK OF WATER
- ■ WATER CONDITION
- ● TEMPERATURE : 26°C
- ● pH VALUE : 7.1
- ● TOTAL HARDNESS (GH) : 4°dH
- ● CARBONATE HARDNESS (KH) : 4°dH
- ● NITRITE (NO_2) : 0.1mg/liter
- ● NITRATE (NO_3) : LESS THAN 10mg/liter
- ● CO_2 : 14mg/liter

THE WORLD OF RYOKAN

When we studied the famous Zen priest and poet Ryokan (1758-1831) in school, we learned that he loved violets, wrote waka, and played with children. He could never wait for spring but went hiking during the thaw, and violets often crop up in his poems from that season. For example, *"Tonight I shall sleep in a field of violets. And if the violets stain my clothes, well, then the violets stain my clothes."*

According to Professor Nagashima of Niigata Seiryo Women's Junior College, those violets Ryokan loved were actually common hepatica. I asked her personally and she has me convinced. As she said, *"Common hepatica is the most beautiful flower commonly found in snowy areas. It is resistant to cold and blooms like mad in the spring."*

They are abundant in Niigata, but the Prefectural Flower is the tulip, which also blooms during the thaw. After the long hard winter, the reds, whites, yellows and blacks of tulip flood the hills of Niigata. I sometimes think that if only there were a windmill, it would be the picture of Holland.

Now I don't mind a foreign flower being made Prefectural Flower, but · since an aquarium with a tulip motif is already known as a Dutch "Datta" aquarium, I propose one that is based on the songs of Ryokan and features common hepatica.

I think perhaps we can discern a difference between Japanese and Western style here. Western aquarists take the colorful aggregation of the flower bed or garden and apply it without adaptation to the aquarium. But Japanese take nature as their starting point.

This unique sense of nature, this wabi-sabi, pervades every aspect of Japanese life, from gardening and bonsai to the tea ceremony and ikebana (flower arrangement) to many aspects of daily life. This is the culture that the Japanese can be proud of. The waterscapes in these pages reflect that culture, and the nature that Ryokan made his pillow.

CATCHING FISH BAREHANDED AFTER A STORM

In the middle of April the snow melts and the plains of Niigata are flooded. This is done intentionally to soften up the rice fields for plowing. When I was a child I would climb up a mountain before sunrise to see the water-covered earth turn into a sheet of gold.

Spring planting time is the happiest season for the farmers in snow country. In the next month the land will be reborn in green. Then in mid-June the rainy season begins and the rice grows quickly. In the old days we didn't have drainage pumps or tunnels, so the levees would break and the fields would quickly fill with water. These were real floods, not like the April flooding, and disturbing as it was to the farmers, we children were thrilled. When the rivers and ponds began to overflow, fat carp would begin to spawn. They would be so distracted that we could catch them by the roadside with our bare hands.

A story we often heard was how the school grounds flooded once during lessons, and from the classroom they could see carp in the water outside the window. Some students couldn't contain themselves anymore and leapt out the window to go catch some. The teachers followed right behind them, and soon most of the school was outside chasing carp and having a great time.

That episode was before my time, but when a heavy rain was falling outside and the class was restless, the teachers would tell us that story, and I think I remember it as well as they do.

Yoroi Wetlands, where the author played as a child (Maki City, Niigata Prefecture, the largest wetlands in the prefecture until it was filled in 1955).
Photo: Yogoeimon Ishiyama

SHOES AND AQUATIC PLANTS

In the post-war days in Japan there were no refrigerators, so people who lived in the interior couldn't eat fresh seafood. Children often caught carp for their families, especially in my home town where we had large wetlands. Our fishing method was a primitive one: we would scoop the water along the banks with a net tied to bamboo poles. A more dangerous way was to dam up the ends of a big submerged pipe, empty out the water with buckets, then climb in to get the fish that remained. Besides fish, hishi, lotus and other plants that the children gathered were an important source of protein. The catch was always divided fairly by paper-scissors-stone, unless we came up with a colorfully displaying tanago (bitterling) or goby, in which case someone would give up their share in order to take home the living beauty. They would carry it home in the rubber shoes we all wore in those days, filled with water for the fish, and the two kilometer walk on a stony road would leave blood blisters on their feet. The feet would make it, bloody though they were, but the fish, due to the heat and lack of oxygen, never did. I was scolded many times for coming home empty-handed. There were many plants in the wetlands that resembled the two-temple and *Hygrophila* that I use today in my waterscapes. The abundant plants (Sasabanohiromo, mizuoobako *(Ottelia)* Matsumo, and Mizuwarabi) were a beautiful sight in the water. And when I broke some off and stuffed them in my shoes, amazingly the fish survived the trip home. Many of my layouts come from childhood memories like this one.

Children gathering lotus roots in Yoroi Wetlands in the late 1950's. (photo by Yogoeimon Ishiyama)

38

DENSE FOREST MELODY

This is a triangular layout designed for appreciation from two angles. This construction strikes a balance between the grassy field in the foreground and the dense forest in the background.

NO. 21 DATA

- ■ PHOTOGRAPHING : JANUARY 1990
- ■ WATER TANK : W550XD550XH550(mm)
- ■ CONTENT : 160 liters
- ■ MAINTENANCE
- ● LIGHTING : 15WX6(90W)
- ● FILTERING : POWER FILTER
- ● SUBSTRATE : AKADAMA CERAMICS
- ● CO_2 SUPPLY : ONCE EVERY THREE SECONDS
- ● FERTILIZATION : 0.1cc/liter
- ● WATER CHANGE : ONCE A WEEK, 1/2 TANK OF WATER
- ■ WATER CONDITION
- ● TEMPERATURE : 25°C
- ● pH VALUE : 7.0
- ● TOTAL HARDNESS (GH) : 2°dH
- ● CARBONATE HARDNESS (KH) : 2°dH
- ● NITRITE (NO_2) : 0.1mg/liter
- ● NITRATE (NO_3) : LESS THAN 10mg/liter
- ● CO_2 : 17mg/liter
- ● O_2 : 7mg/liter

RAINY SEASON

This layout was inspired by the distant memories of swollen rivers during rainy seasons in my childhood. I have only used plants native to Japan, and the fish is the uncommon Japanese baratanago.

NO. 22 DATA

- ■ PHOTOGRAPHING : JUNE 1991
- ■ WATER TANK : W550XD550XH550(mm)
- ■ CONTENT : 160 liters
- ■ MAINTENANCE
- ● LIGHTING : 15WX6(90W)
- ● FILTERING : POWER FILTER
- ● SUBSTRATE : AKADAMA CERAMICS
- ● CO_2 SUPPLY : ONCE EVERY FIVE SECONDS
- ● FERTILIZATION : UNNECESSARY
- ● WATER CHANGE : ONCE A WEEK, 1/2 TANK OF WATER
- ■ WATER CONDITION
- ● TEMPERATURE : 24°C
- ● pH VALUE : 7.0
- ● TOTAL HARDNESS (GH) : 2°dH
- ● CARBONATE HARDNESS (KH) : 3°dH
- ● NITRITE (NO_2) : 0.1mg/liter
- ● NITRATE (NO_3) : LESS THAN 10mg/liter
- ● CO_2 : 19mg/liter
- ● O_2 : 8mg/liter

FRAGRANCE OF SUMMER GRASS

This work represents the thick green foliage of high summer. The lush fragrance that summer grasses exude is invigorating.

NO. 23 DATA

- PHOTOGRAPHING : MAY 1990
- WATER TANK : W550XD550XH550(mm)
- CONTENT : 160 liters
- MAINTENANCE
- LIGHTING : 15W X 6(90W)
- FILTERING : POWER FILTER
- SUBSTRATE : OISO SAND
- CO_2 SUPPLY : ONCE EVERY THREE SECONDS
- FERTILIZATION : 0.1cc/liters
- WATER CHANGE : ONCE EVERY TEN DAYS, 1/2 TANK OF WATER
- WATER CONDITION
- TEMPERATURE : 25°C
- pH VALUE : 7.0
- TOTAL HARDNESS (GH) : 3°dH
- CARBONATE HARDNESS (KH) : 3°dH
- NITRITE (NO_2) : 0.1mg/liter
- NITRATE (NO_3) : LESS THAN 10mg/liter
- CO_2 : 18mg/liter
- O_2 : 9mg/liter

45

LAYOUT TIPS

①

②

③

④

⑤

⑥

⑦

1. To make a layout that will be viewed from two sides, first pile the sand high in the rear and slope it down toward the front. Lay the stones diagonally to fit.

2. Attach some *Bolbitis* onto driftwood using plastic ties. When the "graft" has taken, remove the ties.

3. Considering the best angle for balance, place the driftwood with *Bolbitis* on the rock formation.

4. In order to use the materials we've placed so far to our advantage, avoid planting any large plants in the front.

5. Once most of the elements are in place, add the water gently using a hose and a container below it so as not to make a hole in the sand.

6. While keeping the final product in mind, plant some tall types in the rear corners, such as two-temple and red *Rotala macrantha*.

7. When selecting and locating aquatic plants, it is important to imagine what changes might take place in the future as they grow.

A STROLL THROUGH THE SEA

Using white sea sand, large rocks and *Sagittaria natans* that resembles amamo, this scene is reminiscent of the beautiful South Seas. The peaceful fishes seem to be strolling along without a care.

NO. 24 DATA

- ■ PHOTOGRAPHING : OCTOBER 1991
- ■ WATER TANK : W900XD450XH450(mm)
- ■ CONTENT : 180 liters
- ■ MAINTENANCE
- ● LIGHTING : 30WX3(90W)
- ● FILTERING : POWER FILTER
- ● SUBSTRATE : SEA SAND
- ● CO_2 SUPPLY : ONCE EVERY FIVE SECONDS
- ● FERTILIZATION : UNNECESSARY

THE FALLOW FIELD IS AN AQUATIC PLANT FARM

When the heat of summer passed, cool autumn winds blew, announcing the end of my children's summer vacation. Everyone had played every day, and I occasionally worried like a parent about their homework. But I never actually cracked a book when I was a kid. I can remember going to the mountains at summer's end, and the chirps of the energetic cicadas sounded like "Home-work, home-work, home-work". Like father, like sons.

Summer vacation is the freest time in one's whole life. But children today don't seek adventure and get to

A HOMETOWN STREAM

This is the kind of beautiful stream scene that used to be found everywhere. I used representative native plants to recreate my home town stream. The central plant, mizuoobako, is growing handsomely.

NO. 25 DATA

- ■ PHOTOGRAPHING : JUNE 1990
- ■ WATER TANK : W900XD450XH450(mm)
- ■ CONTENT : 180 liters
- ■ MAINTENANCE
- ● LIGHTING : 30WX4(120W)
- ● FILTERING : POWER FILTER
- ● SUBSTRATE : OISO SAND
- ● CO_2 SUPPLY : ONCE EVERY THREE SECONDS
- ● FERTILIZATION : 0.2cc/liter
- ● WATER CHANGE : ONCE EVERY TWO WEEKS, 1/2 TANK OF WATER
- ■ WATER CONDITION
- ● TEMPERATURE : 22°C
- ● pH VALUE : 6.5
- ● TOTAL HARDNESS (GH) : 3°dH
- ● CARBONATE HARDNESS (KH) : 3°dH
- ● NITRITE (NO_2) : 0.1mg/liter
- ● NITRATE (NO_3) : 10mg/liter
- ● CO_2 : 19mg/liter
- ● O_2 : 8mg/liter

know nature like we did in my youth. For one thing, they are too bound by school rules. Everything has to be chaperoned, so they always have to ask to be taken places. I tell them to just go with their friends, but the school says that's no good.

So we made a family plan again this year. Last year we went to the sea but a typhoon hit so we couldn't swim. To avoid a repeat of that disaster, we decided to climb an over-2000m-high mountain. We stayed in a National Lodge and turned in early so we could get an early start out the next day, but in the middle of the night we were subjected to a heavy storm complete with sky-splitting thunder. The rain hadn't let up by morning. In fact, flood warnings were soon posted and we had to call off the climb. My wife and kids gave me the unaffectionate nickname,"*Rain Man.*"

So we drove down the mountain road in the rain, and gradually a dream-like scene of rice paddies shrouded in rain unfolded before us. Being a shutterbug, I couldn't pass this chance up. Not until I took my eye

from the viewfinder could I see some fallow paddies that were arranged in terraces. I was so absorbed in taking pictures I hadn't noticed them. Excited, I looked closely and saw hair grass, mizuoobako, togerimo, tanukimo, and urikawa, a treasure chest of water plants I hadn't seen for some time. I tore off my shirt and began gathering them.

There were no waves on the leaves of the mizuoobako (*Otrzia*) and they were all small, but so closely packed together! There used to be two species, oomizu and oobako, but now most scholars have combined them into one. But these were somehow different. They were perfect for cultivation and I named the type *himemizuoobako* (Princess Mizuoobako). I figured that this new type I'd found was still growing

strong, but when I returned at the end of summer vacation they were the same size, with flowers.

On that day it was raining, too, so I took off my shirt again to gather specimens. An old man from the neighborhood approached me and told me that he had thought I was a lunatic running loose around the rice paddies half-naked in the rain. We talked for a while, and I learned that the oomizubako wasn't found anywhere else in the neighborhood. I discovered a wide variety of water insects living there (taikoochi, water mantis, and gengorou) and I realized I had a paradise of flora and fauna in my grasp. I asked the man to introduce me to the owner and I begged him to sell it to me. A few days later the owner kindly donated the land to me, and the old man agreed to manage it for me (including water management).

That was the birth of the Japanese Aquatic Plant Research Farm. When I look back now, I realize that the circumstances that led to it hinged at every turn on rain. Now I think that there couldn't be a more fitting nickname for me than "*Rain Man*."

CRIMSON SWORD PLANTS

This waterscape uses only water plants, no driftwood or rocks. The composition is rather uniform, but the crimson sword plants act as an accent and keep the layout from being monotonous.

NO. 26 DATA

- PHOTOGRAPHING : MARCH 1990
- WATER TANK : W900XD450XH450(mm)
- CONTENT : 180 liters
- MAINTENANCE
- LIGHTING : 30W X 4(120W)
- FILTERING : POWER FILTER
- SUBSTRATE : AKADAMA CERAMICS
- CO_2 SUPPLY : ONCE EVERY FIVE SECONDS
- FERTILIZATION : 0.2cc/liters
- WATER CHANGE : ONCE EVERY TWO WEEKS, 1/2 TANK OF WATER
- WATER CONDITION
- TEMPERATURE : 25°C
- pH VALUE : 7.0
- TOTAL HARDNESS (GH) : 3°dH
- CARBONATE HARDNESS (KH) : 2°dH
- NITRITE (NO_2) : 0.1mg/liter
- NITRATE (NO_3) : LESS THAN 10mg/liter
- CO_2 : 16mg/liter
- O_2 : 7mg/liter

PATTERNS OF LEAVES IN WATER

This layout also makes use of the golden section, the main point being the three growths of *Bolbitis* arranged in a scalene triangle in the center. The variously-shaped plants in the background add spice.

NO. 27 DATA

■ PHOTOGRAPHING : FEBRUARY 1989
■ WATER TANK : W900XD450XH600(mm)
■ CONTENT : 240 liters
■ MAINTENANCE
● LIGHTING : 30WX4(120W)
● FILTERING : POWER FILETER
● SUBSTRATE : OISO SAND
● CO_2 SUPPLY : ONCE EVERY FIVE SECONDS

FIVE BOTTLES OF CARBONATED WATER

I decided to make a real effort to raise water plants and design beautiful waterscapes in 1977. At that time there were no power filters and such devices like there are today, and figuring out my first set-up was difficult. I placed about 7cm. of fine coral sand on the bottom and intensely aerated the water with a bottom filter. I thought that putting fishes in would cause problems, so I limited myself to plants. For lighting the 60cm tank I used two 20-watt bulbs: in a week the leaves were yellowing, and in two weeks they were transparent. There were no books to help me out. All I could do was grope on in the dark.

Next I realized that while I could raise plants fairly successfully in old aquaria, the newer ones were just no good. While pondering the reason for this, I figured out that it wasn't just air but CO_2 that they needed, so I asked my mentor, Professor Nagashima of Niigata Seiryo Women's Junior College, about methods for carbonation of aquarium water. He told me that the 0.03% CO_2 in the air should be enough, and that it was naturally absorbed into the water so that I didn't have to add it artificially. But he introduced me to a friend in the medical equipment field anyway, who discussed possible carbonation methods with me and gave me a cost estimate. It's too bad it couldn't have been done more inexpensively or I would have successfully set up an aquatic plant aquarium much sooner. Carbon dioxide was something I never needed in my work and it was too expensive a material for me, anyway. Dry ice was economical, but it was too hard to handle and disappeared too quickly to be practical.

Frustrated, I went on struggling and tried to forget about CO_2. The aquatic plant aquarium work inched along to the point where the plants weren't dying as much but they wouldn't form new buds. Then one night I went to a bar with a friend and a clear bottle of carbonated water caught my eye. The label said, "water, carbon dioxide, sodium chloride (NaCl) 1%." I wasn't sure about the NaCl but it was the perfect material for testing whether the plants needed CO_2. I took five bottles home with me.

The tank for the experiment was big: 240x60x60cm. Flushed with drink and excitement, I poured the five bottles in. Within five minutes air bubbles had formed on the leaves: they did need the CO_2. Every tank I added the soda water to did well, but I had to be careful not to add too much because of that 1% NaCl, and so I changed the water faithfully every week. There were piles of empty soda water bottles all over my room. If I hadn't discovered that carbonated water when I did, I surely would have given up on the whole idea of aquatic plant aquaria.

A PATH THROUGH THE BRUSH

This is another example of a very dense composition.
The foreground space divides the plants into a ratio of
three left to one right, creating the effect of a path
cutting through the brush.

NO. 28 DATA

- ■ PHOTOGRAPHING : DECEMBER 1989
- ■ WATER TANK : W1200XD450XH450(mm)
- ■ CONTENT : 240 liters
- ■ MAINTENANCE
- ● LIGHTING : 40WX2(80W)
- ● FILTERING : ORIGINAL POWER FILTER
- ● SUBSTRATE : OISO SAND
- ● CO_2 SUPPLY : ONCE EVERY FIVE SECONDS
- ● FERTILIZATION : 0.1cc/liter
- ● WATER CHANGE : ONCE EVERY TEN DAYS, 1/2 TANK OF WATER
- ■ WATER CONDITION
- ● TEMPERATURE : 24°C
- ● pH VALUE : 6.8
- ● TOTAL HARDNESS (GH) : 3°dH
- ● CARBONATE HARDNESS (KH) : 3°dH
- ● NITRITE (NO_2) : 0.1mg/liter
- ● NITRATE (NO_3) : 10mg/liter
- ● CO_2 : 17mg/liter
- ● O_2 : 7mg/liter

GROWTH AT THE RIVERHEAD

This waterscape uses only *Cryptocoryne* species. I used rocks gathered from mountain streams to give the impression of a river's source, and added willow moss to give it a little needed warmth.

NO. 29 DATA

- ■ PHOTOGRAPHING : SEPTEMBER 1990
- ■ WATER TANK : W1200XD450XH450(mm)
- ■ CONTENT : 240 liters
- ■ MAINTENANCE
- ● LIGHTING : 40W X 2(80W)
- ● FILTERING : ORIGINAL POWER FILTER
- ● SUBSTRATE : OISO SAND
- ● CO_2 SUPPLY : ONCE EVERY FIVE SECONDS
- ● FERTILIZATION : UNNECESSARY
- ● WATER CHANGE : ONCE A WEEK, 1/3 TANK OF WATER
- ■ WATER CONDITION
- ● TEMPERATURE : 25°C
- ● pH VALUE : 6.8
- ● TOTAL HARDNESS (GH) : 2°dH
- ● CARBONATE HARDNESS (KH) : 1°dH
- ● NITRITE (NO_2) : 0.1mg/liter
- ● NITRATE (NO_3) : LESS THAN 10mg/liter
- ● CO_2 : 16mg/liter
- ● O_2 : 6mg/liter

A BRACING PLAIN

This work is typical of a period when I used only
Echinodorous tenellus. I use a common Japanese
garden style in arranging the Semmi River rocks.

NO. 30 DATA

- ■ PHOTOGRAPHING : OCTOBER 1985
- ■ WATER TANK : W1200XD450XH450(mm)
- ■ CONTENT : 240 liters
- ■ MAINTENANCE
- ● LIGHTING : 20WX4(80W)
- ● FILTERING : POWER FILTER
- ● SUBSTRATE : OISO SAND
- ● CO_2 SUPPLY : ONCE EVERY FIVE SECONDS
- ● FERTILIZATION : UNNECESSARY
- ● WATER CHANGE : ONCE EVERY TWO WEEKS, 1/2 TANK OF WATER
- ■ WATER CONDITION
- ● TEMPERATURE : 26°C
- ● pH VALUE : 6.9
- ● TOTAL HARDNESS (GH) : 2°dH
- ● CARBONATE HARDNESS (KH) : 2°dH
- ● NITRITE (NO_2) : 0.1mg/liter
- ● NITRATE (NO_3) : LESS THAN 10mg/liter
- ● CO_2 : 13mg/liter
- ● O_2 : 6mg/liter

DEEP GREEN BROOK

This aquarium is based on a waterscape I saw near the
Nile River. I used the African plants *Anubias* and
Kurinam, but I needed to use also the non-African
Echinodorus tenellus and *Cryptocoryne costata* in
order to fill out the composition.

NO. 31 DATA

- ■ PHOTOGRAPHING : NOVEMBER 1986
- ■ WATER TANK : W1200XD450XH450(mm)
- ■ CONTENT : 240 liters
- ■ MAINTENANCE
- ● LIGHTING : 40WX2(80W)
- ● FILTERING : ORIGINAL POWER FILTER
- ● SUBSTRATE : OISO SAND
- ● CO$_2$ SUPPLY : DATALESS
- ● FERTILIZATION : UNNECESSARY
- ● WATER CHANGE : ONCE EVERY TWO WEEKS, 1/2 TANK OF WATER
- ■ WATER CONDITION
- ● TEMPERATURE : 25°C
- ● pH VALUE : 7.0
- ● TOTAL HARDNESS (GH) : 3°dH

THE EDGE OF THE RIVER NILE

From the air it is a narrow, green band that winds on and on over the brown land–the Libyan Desert's strip of oasis nourished by the Nile. In March, 1979, I left Cairo alone and travelled the Nile through the Sudan to the Ugandan border, a 5000km trip.

Thirty minutes by car outside of Cairo peppermint farms line the river, and the villages are the picture of medieval Europe's countryside. It reminded me of Van Gogh's "Bridge at Arles."

Pools form along the river bank, and these were covered with a tropical variety of water lily. The atmosphere of the aquarium in the photograph is of the Nile proper, however, specifically the volatile water's edge that can change drastically with a squall or dry spell. At the Nile's edge, these plants are found in the center of thick growths where they receive only indirect sunlight but for a few minutes in the morning when the rising sun is at just the right height.

Besides *anubias*, there was a member of the ine (rice) family that I couldn't identify, so I substituted a similar-looking species, *Echinodorus tenellus*. Designing an aquarium that looks like an African habitat is easy enough, but many of the species are so uncommon that there is no choice but to use similar plants from other areas. It is important not to confuse plants that grow in still waters and plants that grow in running water because the types are completely different.

THOUGHTS ON AFRICA

The Amboseli National Reserve spreads out under the shadow of Mt. Kilimanjaro, and in its confines lions, leopards, and rhinos roam under the watchful eye of the Kenyan government. This was my favorite spot in all of East Africa, because I could see the sun rise from behind Kilimanjaro. I took a lot of photographs of zebras and giraffes running on the plains with the great mountain in the background. It is postcard Africa at its best.

There are many lodges in the park, and they are all designed to blend in with the natural scenery. Not one spoils the atmosphere. The only unsettling thing about them is natural: the lizards that cling to the windows at night, come to feed on the insects that are attracted to the light. A casual glance out the window could bring you face-to-face with some very ugly nightlife.

Most lodges have an artificial pond for attracting wildlife, but the first one I stayed in didn't even have a bath or shower for the human guests, much less one for animals that might drop by. Everything was in the open air except the beds, and I felt like a native.

Next I stayed at a more expensive lodge that had the requisite watering place. All kinds of animals could be viewed because it was the dry season and their usual sources of water were gone. I was fascinated by how different species watered at different times, as if there was a tacit understanding between them. The strongest animals take the best times, so lions and elephants water at their leisure in the cool dusk.

The nocturnals show up when everyone is asleep, of course, so the lodge provides an "animal call service." Guests simply have to inform the lodge what animals they are interested in seeing, and they will be awakened if and when that animal appears at the water hole.

I put in a call for leopards. One night I was awakened by a thunderous roar. I thought it must be a male. I couldn't believe such a sound could be made by an earthly beast. But, in fact, it was coming from quite nearby. I listened more closely and realized what the source was: the American in the next room was snoring. The leopards, perhaps frightened off by my neighbor, never appeared.

I did get to see a lot of other animals come to drink at night, and even animals that I had seen already in the light of day were somehow more mysterious at night. Of course, an animal's behavior varies with its surroundings. A lion drinking at a water hole doesn't act like a lion in the jungle or one on the plain. Weak animals gather in herds on the plain, where they are easy prey for predators. This herding behavior inspired my work "Gathering on the Plain."

FLOWING BETWEEN MOUNTAINS

The plants are in a rock and sand layout that imitates the gentle slope of the foot of a mountain. I went through a time when I particularly enjoyed creating works using this composition of a narrow road leading off into the mountains.

NO. 32 DATA

- ■ PHOTOGRAPHING : APRIL 1987
- ■ WATER TANK : W1200XD450XH450(mm)
- ■ CONTENT : 240 liters
- ■ MAINTENANCE
- ● LIGHTING : 40W X 2(80W)
- ● FILTERING : ORIGINAL POWER FILTER
- ● SUBSTRATE : SEA SAND
- ● CO_2 SUPPLY : ONCE EVERY THREE SECONDS
- ● FERTILIZATION : 0.1cc/liter
- ● WATER CHANGE : ONCE A WEEK, 1/2 TANK OF WATER
- ■ WATER CONDITION
- ● TEMPERATURE : 26°C
- ● pH VALUE : 7.0
- ● TOTAL HARDNESS (GH) : 3°dH
- ● CARBONATE HARDNESS (KH) : 3°dH
- ● NITRITE (NO_2) : 0.1mg/liter
- ● NITRATE (NO_3) : LESS THAN 10mg/liter
- ● CO_2 : 18mg/liter
- ● O_2 : 8mg/liter

SEA BOTTOM

It is an interesting concept, an aquarium based on the sea using freshwater plants and tropical fishes. And the sight of the school of *Corydoras* swimming lazily along the bottom adds humor to the scene.

NO. 33 DATA

- ■ PHOTOGRAPHING : DECEMBER 1989
- ■ WATER TANK : W1200XD450XH450(mm)
- ■ CONTENT : 240 liters
- ■ MAINTENANCE
- ● LIGHTING : 40WX2(80W)
- ● FILTERING : ORIGINAL POWER FILTER
- ● SUBSTRATE : SEA SAND
- ● CO_2 SUPPLY : ONCE EVERY THREE SECONDS, A DROP OF FERTILIZER
- ● FERTILIZATION : UNNECESSARY
- ● WATER CHANGE : ONCE IN A WEEK, 1/2 TANK OF WATER
- ■ WATER CONDITION
- ● TEMPERATURE : 26°C
- ● pH VALUE : 6.8
- ● TOTAL HARDNESS (GH) : 2°dH
- ● CARBONATE HARDNESS (KH) : 1°dH
- ● NITRITE (NO_2) : 0.1mg/liter
- ● NITRATE (NO_3) : LESS THAN 20mg/liter
- ● CO_2 : 16mg/liter
- ● O_2 : 6mg/liter

GATHERING IN THE ROCK GARDEN

The white sand and petrified wood lend lightness to this waterscape. They are balanced nicely by the rather conservatively colored fishes.

NO. 34 DATA

- ■ PHOTOGRAPHING : SEPTEMBER 1991
- ■ WATER TANK : W1200XD450XH450(mm)
- ■ CONTENT : 240 liters
- ■ MAINTENANCE
- ● LIGHTING : 40WX2(80W)
- ● FILTERING : ORIGINAL POWER FILTER
- ● SUBSTRATE : SEA SAND
- ● CO_2 SUPPLY : ONCE EVERY THREE SECONDS
- ● FERTILIZATION : UNNECESSARY
- ● WATER CHANGE : ONCE EVERY TWO WEEKS, 1/2 TANK OF WATER
- ■ WATER CONDITION
- ● TEMPERATURE : 26°C
- ● pH VALUE : 7.0
- ● TOTAL HARDNESS (GH) : 3°dH
- ● CARBONATE HARDNESS (KH) : 2°dH
- ● NITRITE (NO_2) : 0.1mg/liter
- ● NITRATE (NO_3) : LESS THAN 10mg/liter

SCENIC VIEW

This is one of my best works based on the Japanese garden style and using only native Japanese plants. The stemmed plants arranged in orderly fashion in the background have undergone several trimmings in order to produce dense foliage. The fish is the common medaka (*Oryzias latipes*).

NO. 35 DATA

- ■ PHOTOGRAPHING : JUNE 1991
- ■ WATER TANK : W1200XD450XH450(mm)
- ■ CONTENT : 240 liters
- ■ MAINTENANCE
- ● LIGHTING : 20WX8(160W)
- ● FILTERING : POWER FILTER
- ● SUBSTRATE : AKADAMA CERAMICS
- ● CO_2 SUPPLY : ONCE EVERY THREE SECONDS
- ● FERTILIZATION : 0.1cc/liter
- ● WATER CHANGE : ONCE EVERY WEEK, 1/2 TANK OF WATER
- ■ WATER CONDITION
- ● TEMPERATURE : 24°C
- ● pH VALUE : 6.9
- ● TOTAL HARDNESS (GH) : 1°dH
- ● CARBONATE HARDNESS (KH) : 1°dH
- ● NITRITE (NO_2) : 0.1mg/liter
- ● NITRATE (NO_3) : LESS THAN 10mg/liter
- ● CO_2 : 18mg/liter
- ● O_2 : 8mg/liter

FLOWERBEDS VS. NATURE

There are two generally accepted styles of aquarium design: Japanese and European. The European style (with the exception of the Dutch style) is based on European gardens, in which plants are arranged by type in large groups. The main concerns are volume and uniformity. In the Japanese style, however, plants are used sparingly, empty space is utilized, and stones and driftwood are often added. But I use these labels reluctantly.

If asked, I would designate two styles of aquarium design: flowerbed and natural. These would roughly correspond to European and Japanese styles, but these names are more accurate because wonderful examples of natural layouts are found in Europe, and I have seen works that must fall under the flowerbed heading here in Japan. But I'm really not particular about these names. Rather, I hope that aquarists will concentrate on expressing their personal styles and thereby enliven the world of aquaria.

In this Japanese style layout, the plants and fishes are native to Japan, but using the accepted terms the background layout is European style, while the foreground of grass and rocks and open space is Japanese. However, the work as a whole would be considered Japanese by most observers.

What one needs to be particular about is maintaining, that is, trimming, the plants. If that's neglected, then there isn't any style at all, just a wild thicket instead.

MY MOTHER'S NOTEBOOK

 My mother died at age 62 of a blood clot in her brain. Her life was one of constant work and little play, but she truly loved the work of raising produce on the family farm. She was proud of her eggplants and tomatoes, and even as a child I could tell that hers were better than most. Like most farmers in those days she didn't go to school, but she observed the crops every day and recorded her observations in a college notebook.

 In those days, if there was a dry spell or heavy rains, there would always be losses from disease or stunted growth, but we never failed to reap a decent harvest at our farm. The neighbors would come around asking for my mother's "secret," but they always went home disappointed. Oh, she tried to teach them, but she couldn't explain in an afternoon what it took years of patience to understand. Success only needs the awareness of things that other people take for granted. My mother realized this.

 In time, I did my own research on aquatic plants, and learned some "secrets" myself. I think that it's nearly impossible for me to explain them all. I could explain 90% with scientific theory, but the remaining 10% is based on many years of experience and is a kind of intuition that I rely on to help me make decisions under ever-changing conditions. In Japanese there is a word I often use, kandokoro, which means a crucial point that calls for intuition. My intuition is my guide at those key points when answers aren't clear.

 Everyone has intuition, some more than others, usually depending on the amount of experience they have. I've spent many years trying to create the perfect plant aquarium and I'm still failing. Of course, the plants don't die anymore, but I cannot count the number of times I mistook the amount of water to add, or put in too much CO_2 and awoke the next morning to find all the fishes floating dead at the surface. But my intuition grew.

 When a customer compliments my work, I tell them that while it is true that I raise beautiful aquatic plants now, no one has created the same failures again and again more than I have. Most people won't repeat the same failure, but not me. But I can be glad for one thing, and that is that I always keep notes. When I screw up the same thing a number of different ways, then they are at least all good experiences and I gain of lot of practical knowledge from them.

 Thinking back now, so many plants have died by my hand that it's tragic, but something of all of them survives in me, in my intuition. And in my notebooks, in the same way, a part of my mother lives on.

74

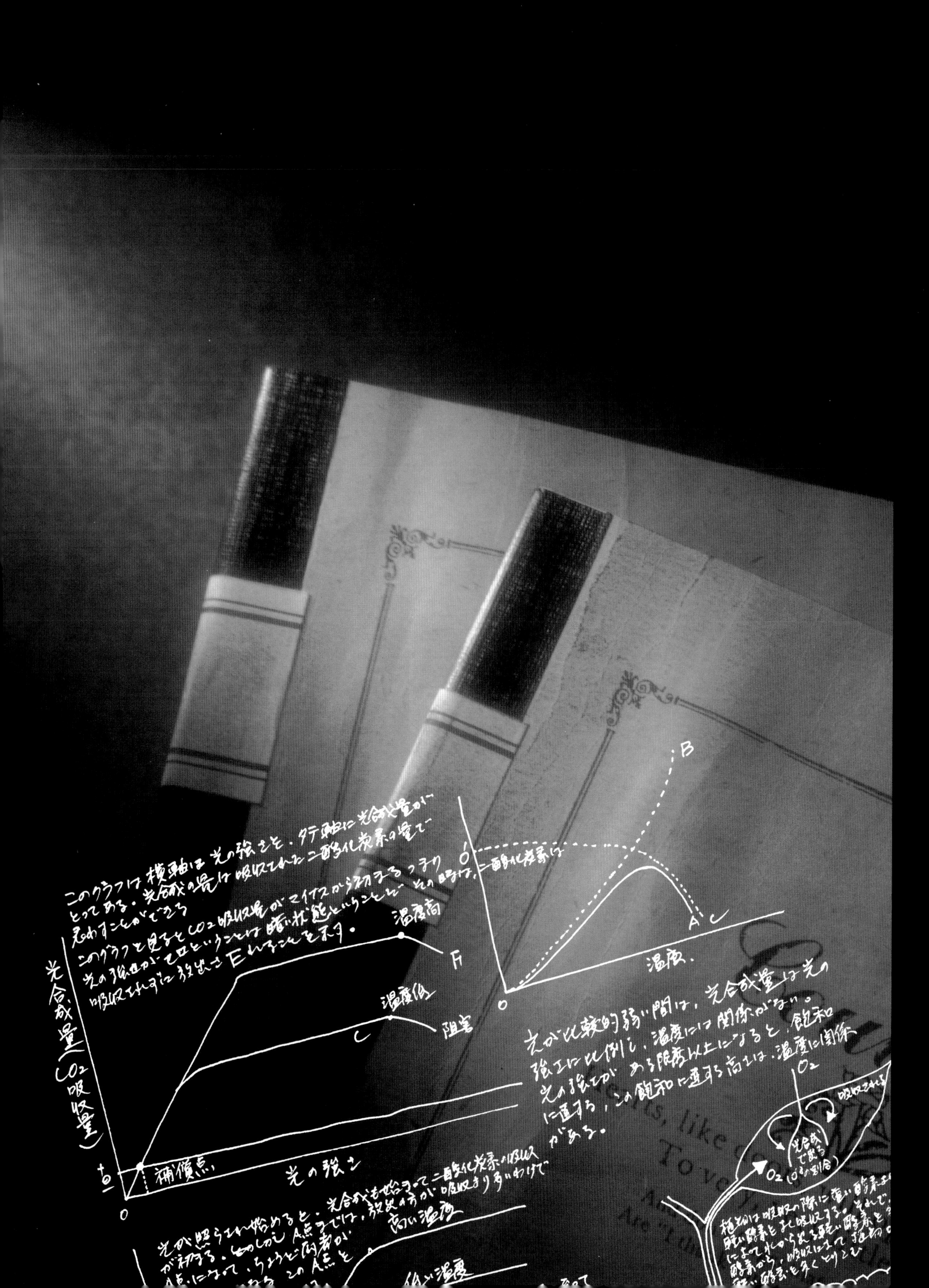

このグラフは 横軸は 光の強さを、タテ軸に光合成量が とってある。光合成の量は吸収された二酸化炭素の量で〜 表わすことができる。

このグラフと見ると CO₂吸収量が マイナスからスタートするグラフ〜 光の強さが ゼロのときには 時いれ話といういことと、それを示すような、二酸化炭素は〜 吸収されずに放出されていることを示す。

光合成量 (CO₂吸収量)

温度高　F

温度低　C

補償点

光の強さ

光が比較的弱い間は、光合成量は光の 強さに比例し、温度には関係がない。 光の強さが ある限度以上になると、飽和 に達する。この飽和に達する高さは、温度に関係 がある。

B

A

温度

O₂

光が照らされ始めると、光合成も始まって二酸化炭素の吸収 が始まる。しかし A点までは、放出する方が 吸収より多いわけで〜 A点になって、ちょうど両者が〜

THE INVISIBLE WATERFALL

This is based on the wabi-sabi atmosphere of a Zen temple garden. The rummy-nose tetras go well with the simplicity of this layout.

NO. 36 DATA

- ■ PHOTOGRAPHING : MAY 1991
- ■ WATER TANK :
  W1500XD450XH600(mm)
- ■ CONTENT : 400 liters
- ■ MAINTENANCE
- ● LIGHTING : 30WX4.20WX4(200W)
- ● FILTERING : POWER FILTER
- ● SUBSTRATE : SEA SAND
- ● CO_2 SUPPLY : ONCE EVERY TWO SECONDS
- ● FERTILIZATION :
- ● WATER CHANGE : ONCE EVERY A WEEK, 1/3 TANK OF WATER
- ■ WATER CONDITION
- ● TEMPERATURE : 26°C
- ● pH VALUE : 7.0
- ● TOTAL HARDNESS (GH) : 2°dH
- ● CARBONATE HARDNESS (KH) : 2°dH
- ● NITRITE (NO_2) : 0.1mg/liter
- ● NITRATE (NO_3) : 10mg/liter
- ● CO_2 : 15mg/liter
- ● O_2 : 5mg/liter

BEHIND THE GREEN CURTAIN

The stillness of a river's surface reflecting the sun of high noon hides this fantastic scene. This aquarium uses six 40-watt bulbs to reproduce daylight.

NO. 37 DATA

- ■ PHOTOGRAPHING : FEBRUARY 1987
- ■ WATER TANK : W1800XD500XH600(mm)
- ■ CONTENT : 540 liters
- ■ MAINTENANCE
- ● LIGHTING : 40WX6(240W)
- ● FILTERING : POWER FILTER
- ● SUBSTRATE : OISO SAND
- ● CO_2 SUPPLY : ONCE EVERY ONE SECOND
- ● FERTILIZATION : UNNECESSARY
- ● WATER CHANGE : ONCE EVERY TWO WEEKS, 1/2 TANK OF WATER
- ■ WATER CONDITION
- ● TEMPERATURE : 26°C
- ● pH VALUE : 6.8
- ● TOTAL HARDNESS (GH) : 2°dH
- ● CARBONATE HARDNESS (KH) : 3°dH
- ● NITRITE (NO_2) : 0.1mg/liter
- ● NITRATE (NO_3) : 10mg/liter
- ● CO_2 : 17mg/liter
- ● O_2 : 6mg/liter

A COLONY OF FERNS

When I set up this aquarium three years ago, the background was full of tall plants, but now they are totally obscured by the ferns. The gouramis seem strangely at home with the ferns.

NO. 38 DATA

- ■ PHOTOGRAPHING : MARCH 1988
- ■ WATER TANK : W1800XD500XH600(mm)
- ■ CONTENT : 540 liters
- ■ MAINTENANCE
- ● LIGHTING : 40WX6(240W)
- ● FILTERING : POWER FILTER
- ● SUBSTRATE : OISO SAND
- ● CO_2 SUPPLY : ONCE EVERY ONE SECOND
- ● FERTILIZATION : UNNECESSARY
- ● WATER CHANGE : ONCE EVERY TWO WEEKS, 1/2 TANK OF WATER
- ■ WATER CONDITION
- ● TEMPERATURE : 26°C
- ● pH VALUE : 7.0
- ● TOTAL HARDNESS (GH) : 3°dH
- ● CARBONATE HARDNESS (KH) : 3°dH
- ● NITRITE (NO_2) : 0.1mg/liter
- ● NITRATE (NO_3) : LESS THAN 20mg/liter
- ● CO_2 : 16mg/liter
- ● O_2 : 5mg/liter

TRANQUIL ENTSUYUI

This design is inspired by the mountain landscapes of China, the native land of the entsuyui (*Myxocyprinus asiaticus*). The simple layout using driftwood in the center is soothing, which is suited to the amusingly calm manner of the fish.

NO. 39 DATA

- ■ PHOTOGRAPHING : DECEMBER 1990
- ■ WATER TANK : W1800XD600XH600(mm)
- ■ CONTENT : 640 liters
- ■ MAINTENANCE
- ● LIGHTING : 40WX6(240W)
- ● FILTERING : ORIGINAL POWER FILTER
- ● SUBSTRATE : OISO SAND
- ● CO_2 SUPPLY : IC. CONTROLLER
- ● FERTILIZATION : UNNECESSARY
- ● WATER CHANGE : ONCE EVERY TWO WEEKS, 1/2 TANK OF WATER
- ■ WATER CONDITION
- ● TEMPERATURE : 26°C
- ● pH VALUE : 6.8
- ● TOTAL HARDNESS (GH) : 3°dH
- ● CARBONATE HARDNESS (KH) : 2°dH
- ● NITRITE (NO_2) : 0.1mg/liter
- ● NITRATE (NO_3) : LESS THAN 10mg/liter
- ● CO_2 : 16mg/liter
- ● O_2 : 5mg/liter

MR. FUJINAMI'S GARDEN

Long ago, the name Muramatsu inspired fear and respect in the land of Echigo (present day Niigata) where that clan ruled. Now the name is more pleasantly associated with Muramatsu Park, which stands on the site of the castle that once overlooked the prosperous surrounding town. The park is famous for the hundreds of large cherry trees that blossom in unison every spring, attracting huge flower-viewing crowds.

A narrow mountain road cuts across a section of the park and leads to a few lovely branches of the Semmi and Hayade Rivers. The clear waters reflect the colors of the seasons, be they the new green buds of spring or the red and yellow leaves of autumn.

The Semmi is the more placid of the two rivers, so it is better for children to swim in. Where this river hits level ground and loses its rapids, there is a wide dry river bed that is perfect for camping and barbecues. Near this river bed is a rest cabin called the Fujisuke Cabin, which is managed by my brother's father-in-law, Harutomo Watanabe. We often meet there and head off to explore the cabin's environs.

He has shown me a lot of wonderful things. For example, when he first introduced me to the beautiful, blackish rocks known as Semmikawa rocks, which I often use in my aquaria, I couldn't believe how perfect they were. Most of the really fine specimens have been snatched up by bonsai and gardening enthusiasts, but many that are good enough for aquarium layouts are still to be found lying about.

There are some deserted villages near the Semmi River. In fact, my sister-in-law was born in a village very deep in the surrounding mountains, and I was surprised how many abandoned homes there were, and how many people used to live in such a remote area. Farthest of all into the mountains is the home of Mr. Fujinami. It is a spacious home made by a skilled carpenter. The original owner was the local landlord. Whoever it was had excellent taste in gardens.

I have seen a lot of famous gardens, and I could go on about this or that technical aspect or school of thought, but this simple garden is perfection. It consists only of some trees, moss, and bamboo grass. And one important element the original builder probably didn't have in mind: time. Time took over and added some wildness to the human construction. I have never seen a garden so perfectly assimilated into the surrounding nature.

The result of the aged garden combined with the mountains in the background and the old home with the thatched roof is pure wabi-sabi. I have visited it many times since that first delightful encounter, and I am always grateful for the warm reception of my gracious host.

DANCING IN THE FOREST

I've created a dense forest by using many plants with broad leaves. The lightly-colored rainbowfish are just the right complement to the subdued colors used in this waterscape.

NO. 40 DATA

- PHOTOGRAPHING : NOVEMBER 1989
- WATER TANK : W1800XD600XH600(mm)
- CONTENT : 640 liters
- MAINTENANCE
- LIGHTING : 40WX6(240W)
- FILTERING : ORIGINAL POWER FILTER
- SUBSTRATE : OISO SAND
- CO_2 SUPPLY : ONCE EVERY ONE SECOND
- FERTILIZATION : UNNECESSARY
- WATER CHANGE : ONCE EVERY TWO WEEKS, 1/2 TANK OF WATER
- WATER CONDITION
- TEMPERATURE : 25°C
- pH VALUE : 7.1
- TOTAL HARDNESS (GH) : 3°dH
- CARBONATE HARDNESS (KH) : 3°dH
- NITRITE (NO_2) : 0.1mg/liter
- NITRATE (NO_3) : LESS THAN 10mg/liter
- CO_2 : 16mg/liter
- O_2 : 6mg/liter

YOUNG LEAVES

Regular trimming causes the long-stemmed plants to grow dense. By leaving a space in the center of the composition, the thick growth is manageable, and the plants can be kept in a kind of esthetic order.

NO. 41 DATA

- ■ PHOTOGRAPHING : JANUARY 1987
- ■ WATER TANK : W1800XD600XH600(mm)
- ■ CONTENT : 640 liters
- ■ MAINTENANCE
- ● LIGHTING : 40WX6(240W)
- ● FILTERING : ORIGINAL POWER FILTER
- ● SUBSTRATE : OISO SAND
- ● CO_2 SUPPLY : ONCE EVERY ONE SECOND, A DROP OF CO_2
- ● FERTILIZATION : 0.1cc/liter
- ● WATER CHANGE : ONCE EVERY TEN DAYS, 1/3 TANK OF WATER
- ■ WATER CONDITION
- ● TEMPERATURE : 26°C
- ● pH VALUE : 7.0
- ● TOTAL HARDNESS (GH) : 1°dH
- ● CARBONATE HARDNESS (KH) : 1°dH
- ● NITRITE (NO_2) : 0.1mg/liter
- ● NITRATE (NO_3) : LESS THAN 10mg/liter
- ● CO_2 : 19mg/liter
- ● O_2 : 8mg/liter

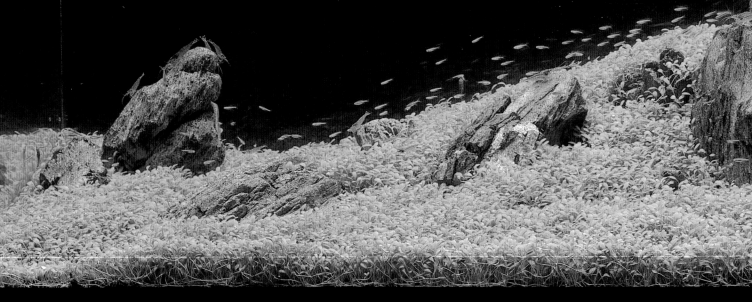

SHINING ON THE PLATEAU

This dynamic layout of petrified wood is unlike the Japanese style of rock arrangement. Instead, I am going for a bright, continental feeling. The thick *Glossostigma* and wood combination presents the cool image of a plateau.

NO. 42 DATA

- ■ PHOTOGRAPHING : DECEMBER 1991
- ■ WATER TANK : W1800XD600XH600(mm)
- ■ CONTENT : 640 liters
- ■ MAINTENANCE
- ● LIGHTING : 40WX4(80W)
- ● FILTERING : POWER FILTER
- ● SUBSTRATE :
- ● CO_2 SUPPLY : ONCE EVERY FIVE SECONDS
- ● FERTILIZATION : 0.1cc/liter
- ● WATER CHANGE : ONCE A WEEK, 1/2 TANK OF WATER
- ■ WATER CONDITION
- ● TEMPERATURE : 27°C
- ● pH VALUE : 6.9
- ● TOTAL HARDNESS (GH) : 1°dH
- ● CARBONATE HARDNESS (KH) : 2°dH
- ● NITRITE (NO_2) : LESS THAN 0.1mg/liter
- ● NITRATE (NO_3) : LESS THAN 10mg/liter
- ● CO_2 : 15mg/liter

GARDEN COLOR SCHEME

This is a new type of work composed of an intricate layout of rocks and plants in a bold design. One important aspect is the fact that Japanese gardening techniques are found throughout the work.

NO. 43 DATA

- ■ PHOTOGRAPHING : OCTOBER 1991
- ■ WATER TANK : W1800XD600XH600(mm)
- ■ CONTENT : 640 liters
- ■ MAINTENANCE
- ● LIGHTING : 20WX16(320W)
- ● FILTERING : ORIGINAL POWER FILTER
- ● SUBSTRATE : OISO SAND
- ● CO_2 SUPPLY : IC. CONTROLLER
- ● FERTILIZATION : 0.1cc/liter
- ● WATER CHANGE : ONCE A WEEK, 1/3 TANK OF WATER
- ■ WATER CONDITION
- ● TEMPERATURE : 25°C
- ● pH VALUE : 7.0
- ● TOTAL HARDNESS (GH) : 2°dH
- ● CARBONATE HARDNESS (KH) : 2°dH
- ● NITRITE (NO_2) : 0.1mg/liter
- ● NITRATE (NO_3) : LESS THAN 20mg/liter
- ● CO_2 : 23mg/liter
- ● O_2 : 9mg/liter

A CARPET OF GREEN

Planted carefully within the carpet of *Riccia* that fills this 180cm tank are accents of hair grass, which grows in the same habitat. Suitable to these native Japanese aquatic plants is the native Japanese freshwater fish mugitsuku (*Pungtungia herzi*).

NO. 44 DATA

- ■ PHOTOGRAPHING : JUNE 1991
- ■ WATER TANK : W1800XD600XH600(mm)
- ■ CONTENT : 640 liters
- ■ MAINTENANCE
- ● LIGHTING : 40WX6(240W)
- ● FILTERING : ORIGINAL POWER FILTER
- ● SUBSTRATE : OISO SAND
- ● CO_2 SUPPLY : ONCE EVERY ONE SECOND
- ● FERTILIZATION : UNNECESSARY
- ● WATER CHANGE : ONCE A WEEK, 1/2 TANK OF WATER
- ■ WATER CONDITION
- ● TEMPERATURE : 24°C
- ● pH VALUE : 6.8
- ● TOTAL HARDNESS (GH) : 1°dH
- ● CARBONATE HARDNESS (KH) : 1°dH
- ● NITRITE (NO_2) : 0.1mg/liter
- ● NITRATE (NO_3) : LESS THAN 10mg/liter
- ● CO_2 : 23mg/liter
- ● O_2 : 9mg/liter

CREATING FROM MEMORY

Memory is interesting. People often can't remember what happened yesterday but can't forget something that happened twenty years ago. When I was a child we didn't have swimming pools. People from the town swam in their district's designated section of the river. The river water was colder than sea or pool water; we could only stand thirty minutes in it before freezing. Then we would stretch out on a wooden bridge to warm up, get bored, and go play in the fields.

Those fields were actually marshlands, and they were covered with a carpet of hair grass (*Eleocharis sp.*) that tickled our bare feet. Puddles were scattered about but they were obscured by floating *Riccia* such that no one could guess they were there. When we played tag, those *Riccia*-covered puddles were the great levelers. If a big kid fell into one up to his waist, even a little kid

could tag him. More than once they saved me from tough older boys when I was the youngest one playing. The green "rugs" protected me, I thought, like they protected the frogs and insects that hid in them.

Those two marvelous species, hair grass and *Riccia*, grew wild in the same marsh. They were beautiful to a child's eyes, but I hadn't thought about them for thirty years, until today as I tried to recreate the memory of those days in a waterscape, and the pictures reappeared vividly on my mind's screen. The result is a kind of mirror image, for in this work hair grass is scattered among the *Riccia*.

Incidentally, I also recall what we used to call hair grass (a fine name for the species). We called it *ushi-koge*, which means "cow brush" because it looked like the scrub brush we used to clean cows.

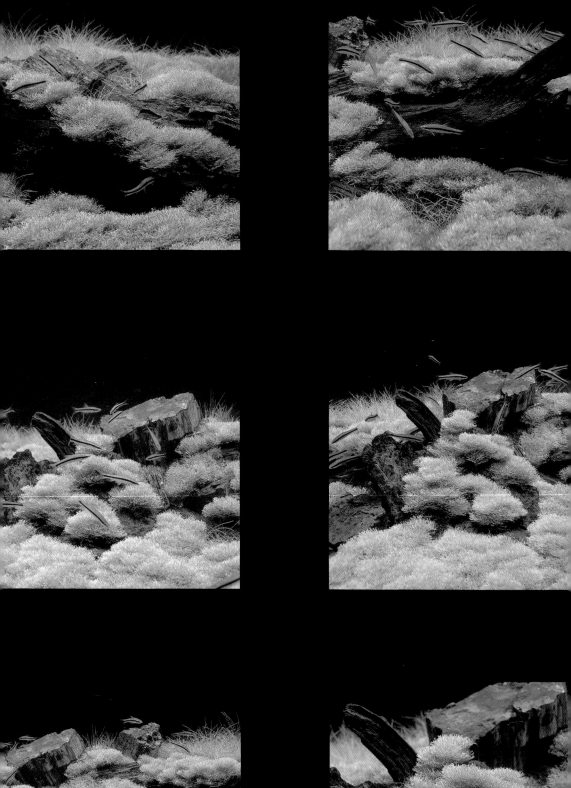
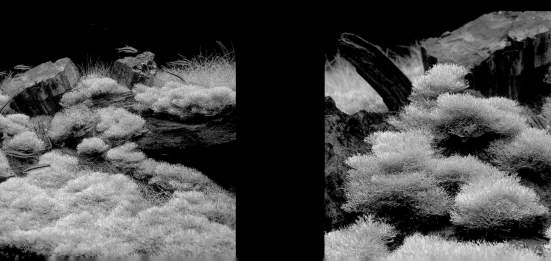

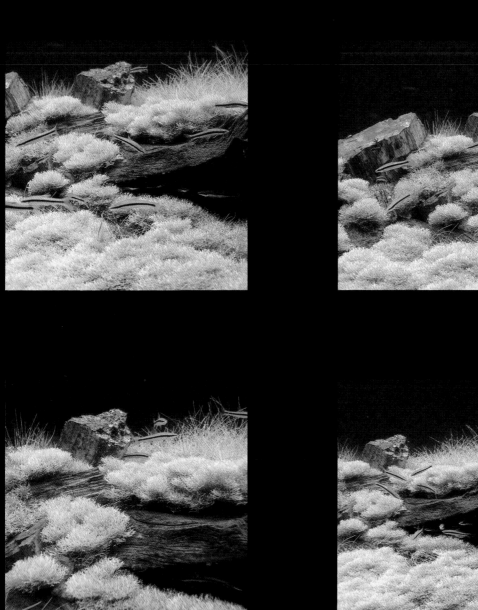

SEEING GREATNESS IN LITTLE THINGS

I am not a member of a Zen sect but I do have an
interest in it, and I have spent time at a Zen temple in
Shizuoka Prefecture. Twice a day, morning and
evening, we did an hour of zazen, or sitting meditation,
so my ten week-long visits give me a total of 140 hours
of zazen experience. That is still pretty far from
removing the illusory veil of reality and knowing
enlightenment, believe me.

Zen was imported from China in the Kamakura Era
(1192-1333), and the priest Eisai is famous for bringing
the teachings to Japan. The influence Zen has exerted
on Japan since then is immeasurable. My greatest
interest is in Zen gardens, and though I'm self-taught,
I've managed to acquire a substantial knowledge of
them through reading and visiting the gardens
themselves.

The best known example of Zen garden style is
probably the kare-sansui, usually translated as
"invisible waterfall." Using only rocks and wood, it tries
to produce the illusion of rushing water out of thin air.
This technique became popular during the Muromachi
Era (1338-1573) as an innovative way to evoke the
great mountain streams of China in a garden of limited
space.

I also try to imitate the vastness of nature in the limited
spaces of my aquaria. The method of the invisible
waterfall seeks to "express a whole universe in a small
space." It allows the viewer to "see greatness in little
things," as Zen teaches, and these ideas motivate my
own work. Some of the invisible waterfall gardens that
have especially influenced the rock and plant
arrangements in my work can be found at famous
temples in Kyoto and Nara like Daitokuji and Ryuan-ji. I
also find the words of Shoshu Tachihara, from his book
Japanese Gardens, illuminating:

*"Europeans have always believed that beauty is
something people create, while Easterners have
always incorporated nature's beauty into their daily
lives. I visited a few palace gardens in Europe. They
were just decorations. The carefully sectioned flower
beds left me cold. The famous Zen garden at Ryuan-ji
may also be considered abstract, since it uses only
rocks and sand. Yet these primal elements of nature
are transformed into beautiful art. Clearly the basic
concepts of gardening are completely different in the
East and West."*

DIPPED IN GREEN

The dark green leaves of *Anubias nana* highlight the dense forest of aquatic plants. The lone platy in the center adds a bright brushstroke of color.

NO. 45 DATA

- ■ PHOTOGRAPHING : OCTOBER 1991
- ■ WATER TANK : W2250XD450XH600(mm)
- ■ CONTENT : 600 liters
- ■ MAINTENANCE
- ● LIGHTING : 30WX4.2WX8(280W)
- ● FILTERING : POWER FILTER
- ● SUBSTRATE : OISO SAND
- ● CO_2 SUPPLY : ONCE EVERY ONE SECOND
- ● FERTILIZATION : 0.1cc/liter
- ● WATER CHANGE : ONCE EVERY TWO WEEKS, 1/2 TANK OF WATER
- ■ WATER CONDITION
- ● TEMPERATURE : 26°C
- ● pH VALUE : 6.9
- ● TOTAL HARDNESS (GH) : 3°dH
- ● CARBONATE HARDNESS (KH) : 2°dH
- ● NITRITE (NO_2) : 0.1mg/liter
- ● NITRATE (NO_3) : LESS THAN 20mg/liter
- ● CO_2 : 18mg/liter

MICROSORIUM ON IRIOMOTE ISLAND

I have visited Iriomote Island, famous since the discovery of the Iriomote wildcat, three times in the late 1970's. Tourists in great numbers followed close after the new fame of this primitive island, which has been called Japan's final frontier. A sightseeing industry had sprung up on the east side of the island, with regular boat excursions to the neighboring Ishigaki Island, and women in high heels and men in suits had become a common sight.

I passed through the east side but never stopped to visit. A bus took me down the two-thirds finished island road to the last stop. From there I chartered a boat to a village which was surrounded by such steep cliffs that a road to it could not be built. In fact, this island within an island could not be reached even on foot from the nearest village. A total population of twenty persons lived in the village's six houses, each equipped with home generators for electricity. Of course the village had no running water, and everyone drank water that was filtered using jasmine tea. Since the community had to be self-sufficient, the tasks of survival were shared. They fished together, hunted wild boar together, and gathered mountain vegetables together. I immediately fell in love with the place and the village head agreed to let me lodge with him. My day there began early with fishing. From time to time schools of aigo (rabbitfishes) or halfbeak would come along and I could catch a lot of them, but my real targets were butterflyfish, angelfishes, or gobies, which were common. I used the tails of hermit crabs as bait, and every hour I would catch one or two interesting fishes that were unlike anything listed in the species charts.

After breakfast I would take some nigiri rice with me and spend the rest of the day in the jungle. At first I was frightened and would not venture very far, but as the days wore on I became accustomed to the area and travelled deeper and deeper into the bush. My biggest fear was snakes, and there was no shortage of them around. There was abundant reptile life, as well as rare species of eagle, pigeon, and bat I had known previously from endangered species lists.

In that treasure chest of rare species, my greatest interest was ferns. I saw many different species, and I was collecting their roots when I came across some *Microsorium*, the popular plant for tropical fishes, growing in a mountain stream. There wasn't a great deal, just some plants here and there clinging to wet rocks, but it had never been found wild in Japan before.

After I returned home, I told the great aquatic plant authority Mitsuo Yamazaki about my discovery. Later he asked me to tell him the exact location since he was going to make an expedition to the island. A few years later, he mentioned the habitat in his *Iriomote Island Expedition Diary*.

THE POISONOUS POTATOS OF YONAKUNI ISLAND

Yonakuni Island is a solitary island out in the East China Sea, located about 500km southwest of Okinawa and only 150km from Taiwan, which I visited twice in the late 1970's. There were two villages on the island, and a bus ran between them twice a day. At that time, the bus hadn't been inspected and the driver had no license. When I asked some of the locals about that, they angrily responded that they didn't have those kinds of things there. I soon realized that there wasn't even police or a doctor on this quiet island.

I stayed there for two weeks, and was fascinated by the fact that even though it was in the same Yaeyama group of islands as Iriomote and Ishigaki, the geography and wildlife were completely different. The many steep cliffs and the deep blue skies made for beautiful scenery, but the atmosphere of the island was tinged with the sadness of its history. I stayed at an inn in Sonai village and explored some nearby caves that even the villagers hadn't entered, and caught some yashigani (crabs). I also found eels as big as a man's arm, large specimens of crabs and insects, and spent my days happily photographing and collecting samples.

One day I headed out for the unexplored area of the island. I walked about ten kilometers through mainly old-growth forest. At some point I stopped to rest on a large boulder. I lost myself in the nature around me. Some butterflies and birds were drinking from puddles on the boulder. Overhead large ferns loomed, and there were some orchids whose name I didn't know. The plant life seemed to be typical of tropical zones, nothing out of the ordinary. But I was given some ideas about how to use tropical plants in my aquaria.

Suddenly I felt extremely hungry, but to my utter dismay I had forgotten my lunch, of all things. Then I noticed the white, cut ends of wild potatos where I had just hacked with my hatchet to clear the trail. I recalled the potatos I had seen at breakfast at the inn that looked so delicious, and how the old woman had told me that they grew all over the mountains.

I cut one into bite-sized pieces and began to wolf it down, but a terrible acrid taste filled my mouth and I started gulping water. However, in a moment I couldn't even keep water in my numb mouth, and then I knew these were bad potatos. But in a kind of shock, I just continued on to the canyon I was heading for, suffering the whole time. I have photos from that canyon I don't remember taking. When I got back to the inn, the owner knew instantly that I had eaten poisonous potatos, but my mouth wouldn't work and I could not answer his questions. All I could do was drool.

The next day I was flown by Cessna to the hospital on Ishigaki Island. A doctor and three nurses attended to me, but I was still unable to answer questions. My mouth burned as if I had drunk boiling water.

"So you've eaten some birugasa," said a nurse. I nodded. "I've always been told to stay away from it," she continued. "They said that just touching it could make you go crazy, the poison is so strong. Even cows and mice won't eat it!"

All of them were turning away from me and unsuccessfully attempting to stifle their laughter. I tried to say something, but just saliva and tears came out. It was pathetic.

The doctor turned to me and said, "We've never had a patient with this condition. We must keep you around for observation a while. Don't worry about fees, it's on us."

His eyes were tearing like mine were, but from trying to contain his laughter.

103

GATHERING ON THE PLAIN

This waterscape is based on the savannah. The
elements of the composition (driftwood, river rocks,
Echinodorus tenellus, *Cryptocoryne wendtii*, and willow
moss) seem to add up to a dull work, but the cardinal
tetra is the key ingredient which gives it an invigorating
coolness.

NO. 46 DATA

- ■ PHOTOGRAPHING : DECEMBER 1990
- ■ WATER TANK : W2400XD600XH600(mm)
- ■ CONTENT : 860 liters
- ■ MAINTENANCE
- ● LIGHTING : 40WX6(240W)
- ● FILTERING : ORIGINAL POWER FILTER
- ● SUBSTRATE : OISO SAND
- ● CO_2 SUPPLY : ONCE EVERY ONE SECOND
- ● FERTILIZATION : UNNECESSARY
- ● WATER CHANGE : ONCE EVERY TWO WEEKS, 1/2 TANK OF WATER
- ■ WATER CONDITION
- ● TEMPERATURE : 26°C
- ● pH VALUE : 6.9
- ● TOTAL HARDNESS (GH) : 2°dH
- ● CARBONATE HARDNESS (KH) : 2°dH
- ● NITRITE (NO_2) : 0.1mg/liter
- ● NITRATE (NO_3) : LESS THAN 10mg/liter
- ● CO_2 : 16mg/liter
- ● O_2 : 6mg/liter

SCENT OF GREEN WIND

This is an example of a U-shaped layout, with a large amount of driftwood and plants on the sides, and open space in the center and foreground. A comparison of the photos at six months and one year post-planting reveals how the plants grew into the design.

NO. 47 DATA

- ■ PHOTOGRAPHING : APRIL 1986
- ■ WATER TANK : W2400XD600XH600(mm)
- ■ CONTENT : 860 liters
- ■ MAINTENANCE
- ● LIGHTING : 40WX6(240W)
- ● FILTERING : ORIGINAL POWER FILTER
- ● SUBSTRATE : SEA SAND
- ● CO_2 SUPPLY : IC. CONTROLLER
- ● FERTILIZATION : 0.1cc/liter

- ● WATER CHANGE : ONCE EVERY TEN DAYS, 1/3 TANK OF WATER
- ■ WATER CONDITION
- ● TEMPERATURE : 26°C
- ● pH VALUE : 6.8
- ● TOTAL HARDNESS (GH) : 2°dH
- ● CARBONATE HARDNESS (KH) : 3°dH
- ● NITRITE (NO_2) : 0.1mg/liter
- ● NITRATE (NO_3) : LESS THAN 20mg/liter
- ● CO_2 : 15mg/liter
- ● O_2 : 5mg/liter

GAIA UNDER GLASS

Everyone is aware of the grave enviromental problems we face now, such as pollution and global warming, but it is not a simple matter of increased CO_2 from industrialization in the atmosphere. Massive deforestation for farming and follies like golf courses, and the destruction of coral reefs through ocean pollution are two examples of how adults

forget what every junior high school student knows: the important connection between CO_2 and plant life.

The importance of plants to animal life cannot be overestimated. Besides producing oxygen, plants emit antibiotics that destroy harmful viruses and bacteria. Aquarists can witness the connection between the two kingdoms of life. When the aquarium plants are healthy, the fishes are healthy. When the balance is lost and the plants stop growing, trouble starts. White spot disease breaks out. Algae grows all over everything and there is a bad smell. An enviromental disaster has occurred in the tank.

Of course, it is shortages of CO_2 that cause problems for aquatic plants. They thrive too much and suddenly there isn't enough CO_2 to go around. Aquarists can buy CO_2 when they need more, and there are high-tech computer chip control systems available. The easy availability of packaged CO_2 has sparked technological progress in aquatic plant aquariums.

This 240x60x60cm tank is equipped with a computerized pH controller that is sensitive to the hundredth place. It releases CO_2 when the pH rises as a result of photosynthesis, and halts at the pre-set optimum level. At night, when the pH goes down, the air pump switches on to raise it back up. This is total technological control.

In the top photo, there are no fishes swimming around. That's because they are all dead, killed in a high-tech accident. The computer sensor had moved out of the water so its readings were all wrong, and it pumped CO_2 into the tank all through the night before the shooting. Total technological control is convenient, until it leads to a total disaster. Earth isn't an aquarium, but the high-tech revolution is leading toward that kind of control, that kind of power, and that kind of risk.

SCHOOL COLORS

This watercape is based on a branch of the Amazon River. A school of 500 colorful cardinal tetras swim through a jungle of *Echinodorus horemanii* and *Microsorium*.

NO. 48 DATA

- ■ PHOTOGRAPHING : SEPTEMBER 1989
- ■ WATER TANK : W2400XD600XH600(mm)
- ■ CONTENT : 860 liters
- ■ MAINTENANCE
- ● LIGHTING : 40WX6(240W)
- ● FILTERING : ORIGINAL POWER FILTER

- ● SUBSTRATE : OISO SAND
- ● CO_2 SUPPLY : ONCE EVERY ONE SECOND
- ● FERTILIZATION : 0.1cc/liter
- ● WATER CHANGE : ONCE EVERY TWO WEEKS, 1/2 TANK OF WATER
- ■ WATER CONDITION
- ● TEMPERATURE : 25°C
- ● pH VALUE : 6.9
- ● TOTAL HARDNESS (GH) : 2°dH
- ● CARBONATE HARDNESS (KH) : 3°dH
- ● NITRITE (NO_2) · 0.1mg/liter
- ● NITRATE (NO_3) : LESS THAN 10mg/liter
- ● CO_2 : 18mg/liter
- ● O_2 : 9mg/liter

DRIFTWOOD SHADOWS

The base structure is a V-shaped arrangement of driftwood on which is planted willow moss and ferns. The lighting emphasizes the dark foreground, which is shadowed by the driftwood, and the light background growth. This was a totally new type of layout that came to me one day in a flash of inspiration.

NO. 49 DATA

- ■ PHOTOGRAPHING : MAY 1986
- ■ WATER TANK : W2400XD600XH600(mm)
- ■ CONTENT : 860 liters
- ■ MAINTENANCE
- ● LIGHTING : 40WX6(240W)
- ● FILTERING : ORIGINAL POWER FILTER
- ● SUBSTRATE : SEA SAND
- ● CO_2 SUPPLY : IC. CONTROLLER
- ● FERTILIZATION : UNNECESSARY
- ● WATER CHANGE : ONCE EVERY TWO WEEKS, 1/2 TANK OF WATER
- ■ WATER CONDITION
- ● TEMPERATURE : 26°C
- ● pH VALUE : 6.8
- ● TOTAL HARDNESS (GH) : 2°dH
- ● CARBONATE HARDNESS (KH) : 1°dH
- ● NITRITE (NO_2) : 0.1mg/liter
- ● NITRATE (NO_3) : LESS THAN 10mg/liter
- ● CO_2 : 17mg/liter
- ● O_2 : 6mg/liter

THE IDEAL ALGAE MUNCHER

 Before the yamato-numaebi (shrimp) appeared in tropical fish aquaria as an algae-control agent, the algae that invariably infested the tank after planting was a great pain in the neck. The aquarium in the photo is clear now, but when I had first set it up, it looked like an algae exhibition tank.

 I like to experiment with different combinations of organisms in aquaria. I've learned that viviparous fishes, like the black molly or swordtail, take care of the soft algae-like tangle; scats best handle hard, calcareous algae; *Otocinclus* or dappled shell is great for light brown algae. By trial and error I learned how to deal with algae, and shrimp are easily the most effective animals. At first I was amazed at the way they would dig into even hard algae.

 Then one day I met a freshwater fish dealer and asked

sensitive to heat. But there was a special, beautiful shrimp in a plastic bag with the name yamato-numaebi written on it in red marker. That shrimp averaged nearly a hundred on my tests. On its report card I wrote, "The best living thing for dealing with algae in an aquarium," and sent a fax asking the dealer to collect a few thousand more for me.

 The dealer was not enthusiastic. He said that that shrimp didn't sell, that he had just recently unloaded a few hundred old-timers, and now I was asking him to collect a few thousand more? I had to convince him. I told him he would soon be selling so many thousands of yamato-numaebi that he'd be going crazy. I told him I would buy whatever he collected until word got around, because I could definitely sell them. I asked him not to sell to any other dealer no matter how good

WATER GREEN FISH

A stand of wisteria runs through the center of this composition. The slight cloudiness in the left side of the photo is a result of the heavy plant growth, which is more than the filtration system can handle.

NO. 50 DATA

- ■ PHOTOGRAPHING : NOVEMBER 1981
- ■ WATER TANK : W2400XD600XH600(mm)
- ■ CONTENT : 860 liters
- ■ MAINTENANCE
- ● LIGHTING : 40WX8(320W)
- ● FILTERING : POWER FILTER
- ● SUBSTRATE : OISO SAND
- ● CO_2 SUPPLY : ONCE EVERY ONE SECOND, A DROP OF CO_2
- ● FERTILIZATION : A LITTLE
- ● WATER CHANGE : ONCE A WEEK, 1/3 TANK OF WATER
- ■ WATER CONDITION
- ● TEMPERATURE : 28°C
- ● pH VALUE : 6.9
- ● TOTAL HARDNESS (GH) : 3°dH
- ● CARBONATE HARDNESS (KH) : 2°dH
- ● NITRITE (NO_2) : 0.1mg/liter
- ● NITRATE (NO_3) : LESS THAN 20mg/liter
- ● CO_2 : 19mg/liter

A BRUSH WITH DEATH AT SEA

Everyone who grew up with Robinson Crusoe as I did has dreamed of adventures on a deserted island. When I grew tired of my lessons, I would open an atlas and imagine journeys through distant seas. Of all the colors of the world map, the green of the plains, the sepia of the mountains, the light brown of the deserts, it was the marine blue of the sea that captured me.

Ten years later, I was at an inn on Ishigaki Island on my bed reading Tetsuo Takara's *Dialogues with Nature*, a collection of the scholar's observations of the nature of the Yaeyama Islands in a simple journal style. In it he mentions an unexplored Nakanokami Island, and I read on as follows: "The waters around Nakanokami are abundant with fishes; it is a sea bird's feeding paradise. The currents around the island are strong enough to give rise to whirlpools, and in inclement weather, travel to it is ill-advised. There have been several accidents by boaters wishing to observe flocks of sea fowl, so extreme caution is necessary."

An electric current of excitement passed through my body upon reading this. I had to go to that island! Within a few minutes I was asking around the docks, but no one was willing to let me charter their boat to such a dangerous area. But I was young, and the more dangerous it sounded, the more I wanted to go. I tried the neighboring Iriomote Island, but it was the same story: "Not for all the money in Tokyo."

Having tried everything else, I hopped the six-hour boat from Ishigaki to Hateruma, the closest island to Nakanokami. Luckily, I ran into a master fisherman named Inoue, who put me up in his home. When I told him my wish, he said he would take me if the right weather came along. I spent a week waiting, a long time on an island small enough to see everything in three hours.

On the last day he woke me up, saying, "Come on, come on. Today's a day we can't pass up." I put my camera, a change of clothes, and food in plastic bags in a cooler as he instructed. The boat was a newly-renovated five meter fiberglass model that was fast but unstable. Going out the waves were about five meters high, but since they were behind us we handled them fine. On the way we caught a two meter mackerel by the primitive method of trolling.

About an hour out, we sighted a distant battleship of a boulder. As we approached, whirlpools spun in the water and huge flocks of waterfowl flew around the island, just as the book said. We pulled into the perfectly semicircular harbor, which was calm, and cut the engine. Mr. Inoue told me that he couldn't take the ship any closer so I would have to swim the rest of the way. I tore off my clothes and was about to plunge into the water when he stopped me, saying, "Hold on! There might be sharks."

He peered out into the water for a while, then with a satisfied look, he said, "OK," and pushed me in.

The cooler was tied to my waist, and I kept thinking of the movie "Jaws." Below me in the clear water I could see napolean and large daibu lolling about. Then dozens of scabbard fish (tachiuo) came along, and the sky above us darkened with birds.

The shore was pockmarked with the dug nests of petrel, and was hard to walk on. Since the wind was strong, the island was covered with sargassum plants. I sat and ate my nigiri rice, and was just about to set off exploring when I heard Inoue yelling. He sounded urgent as he stood in the boat pointing at the sky, so I headed back. When I climbed on board, he said, "Be prepared for a rough trip," and he wrapped me in some foul weather gear and tied a lifeline to me.

I thought he was exaggerating the danger, and naturally I was upset that I hadn't had a chance to see the island, but within an hour the waves had tripled in size, the sky was dark, and a sidelong rain pelted our faces. The ship plummeted down waves like mountains into dark valleys of water. In an unsteady boat in already unsafe waters we had run into a 'Taiwanese monk,' slang for a tropical low pressure.

Just when I was starting to resign myself to the fact that I might not make it back and I hadn't even explored the island, my eyelids brightened and I opened my eyes to see a ray of light breaking through the clouds. Over my head, there were flashes of blue-silver in the narrow sunlight: hundreds of flying fish were soaring over the ship. Out in the sea, some sliced into the swells and some flew over. They were beautiful, with their transparent pectoral fins and their scales glinting in the light. This scene was a gift, and I promised myself I would tell everyone about it if I returned alive.

March, 1975

PUSHING UP DAISIES

The whole composition is structured around the
magnificent specimen of driftwood laid in the center.
The tiger red lotus on the right side may strike some as
off-balance, but it is just right for this scraggy driftwood.

NO. 51 DATA

- ■ PHOTOGRAPHING : NOVEMBER 1985
- ■ WATER TANK : W2400XD750XH750(mm)
- ■ CONTENT : 1350 liters
- ■ MAINTENANCE
- ● LIGHTING : 40WX8(320W)
- ● FILTERING : POWER FILTER (X4)
- ● SUBSTRATE : OISO SAND
- ● CO_2 SUPPLY : ONCE EVERY ONE SECOND
- ● FERTILIZATION : 0.1cc/liter
- ● WATER CHANGE : ONCE EVERY TWO WEEKS, 1/2 TANK OF WATER
- ■ WATER CONDITION
- ● TEMPERATURE : 26°C
- ● pH VALUE : 6.9
- ● TOTAL HARDNESS (GH) : 3°dH
- ● CARBONATE HARDNESS (KH) : 3°dH
- ● NITRITE (NO_2) : 0.1mg/liter
- ● NITRATE (NO_3) : LESS THAN 20mg/liter
- ● CO_2 : 18mg/liter
- ● O_2 : 6mg/liter

"KEEPING TROPICAL FISH IS SIMPLE, ISN'T IT!"

Once I was asked to install an aquarium in a new restaurant on the national highway that runs through the Niigata plain, and it sounded like a great job at first, until I got the details. The restaurant was going to open on August 15, the Festival of the Lanterns, or o-bon holiday, but the construction wouldn't be completely finished until the 14th, so that gave me from the evening of the 14th to around noon on the 15th to finish everything. The tank was 240x75x75cm, not so huge, so I unthinkingly agreed. Then the designer dropped the bombshell.

"Oh yeah, there's going to be an opening ceremony on the 15th, in the early evening. The water will be all clear by then, right? I think about ten different types of tropical fish should do it. Your aquarium is the centerpiece of the restaurant, so we'd like everything perfect, all right? Thank you so much."

I immediately regretted agreeing to such a ridiculous timetable. I had to put in the tank, set it up and fill it, plant the plants, and put in the fishes in under 18 hours. And they wanted the water clear and the whole aquarium to look good enough for a ceremony, not like a tank that had just been set up. This was nearly impossible. And most of the people at the ceremony would have no idea what it takes to make an aquarium look good, how it needs time to settle in.

In the end it worked out all right. I set up the aquarium in time, three hours on the tank, filter, and bottom, ten hours on the plants and details. And this under poor working conditions: no air conditioning, the windows didn't open, and no assistant because I had to cut back on help before this job.

The clarity of the water was about 70% at the start of the ceremony, but by the end it was more like 90%. The trick was to use four Fluval filters: two carbon chemical filters, and two sensitive biological fliters that are used on already clean water. Finally, just to make doubly sure, I poured the bottom sand through large nets to sift out any detritus. The water cleared up in record time, and not only did not a single fish die, in no time they were swimming around as happily as if they'd been born there.

At the ceremony I was exhausted from working through most of the night before. The toasts went right to my head, and pretty soon I was dozing in my seat. I can remember hearing some of the conversation around me as I faded away: "Boy, those tropical fish are pretty." "Can you just put the fish in right after setting up the aquarium?" "Keeping tropical fish is easy, isn't it!"

1. Kikage Coffee Shop.
2. Mitsukoshi Department Store at Bandai.
3. The author's study.
4. Vichyssoise Restaurant.
5. The Shiga Residence.

WRAPPED IN DEEP GREEN

This aquarium can be viewed from both the front and back. Ample space is left open in the foreground, and a piece of driftwood is used on each side. The roots of the *anubias* dangling from the driftwood look very natural.

NO. 52 DATA

- ■ PHOTOGRAPHING : JUNE 1989
- ■ WATER TANK : W1400XD800XH800(mm)
- ■ CONTENT : 890 liters
- ■ MAINTENANCE
- ● LIGHTING : 40WX6(240W)
- ● FILTERING : ORIGINAL POWER FILTER
- ● SUBSTRATE : OISO SAND
- ● CO_2 SUPPLY : IC. CONTROLLER
- ● FERTILIZATION : UNNECESSARY
- ● WATER CHANGE : ONCE EVERY TWO WEEKS, 1/3 TANK OF WATER
- ■ WATER CONDITION
- ● TEMPERATURE : 25°C
- ● pH VALUE : 6.8
- ● TOTAL HARDNESS (GH) : 2°dH
- ● CARBONATE HARDNESS (KH) : 1°dH
- ● NITRITE (NO_2) : 0.1mg/liter
- ● NITRATE (NO_3) : LESS THAN 10mg/liter
- ● CO_2 : 17mg/liter
- ● O_2 : 6mg/liter

RAINY SEASON

This is based on West African waterscapes, specifically the shorelines that are swollen with water during the rainy season. They are difficult to see but the aquarium is full of dwarf cichlids.

NO. 53 DATA

- ■ PHOTOGRAPHING : DECEMBER 1985
- ■ WATER TANK : W1200XD1000XH750(mm)
- ■ CONTENT : 900 liters
- ■ MAINTENANCE
- ● LIGHTING : 20WX10(200W)
- ● FILTERING : POWER FILTER (X2)
- ● SUBSTRATE : SEA SAND

A FISH AT HOME IS A BEAUTIFUL FISH

One of the most enjoyable times for aquarists is when the difficult work of setting up an aquarium is finished and they can contemplate on what fish to raise in it. There is another kind of satisfaction when, as in this case, the aquarium is being built for a certain species. A lot of time and energy must be put into creating just the right atmosphere for the fish. But the rewards equal the efforts, and the thrill of seeing that fish reproduce is well worth it.

This is a really strange waterscape. The usual aquarium is designed with the intention of displaying the fish. What we have here are opportunities for the fish to hide or, we hope, to show themselves. This design came about in reaction to two troubling aspects of the dwarf cichlid's personality: it is very shy and shuns open water; and despite its size, it is a vicious fighter during spawning season and it will attack both strange fishes and its own kind.

With these things in mind, I first decided on a piece of driftwood that had two overhanging branches, and then made a pyramid of river rocks in the center. The pyramid imitates the interior of the pyramid at Giza. That is, the inside of the rockpile is a maze, so the fish should be able to avoid each other as they hide out. However, I illuminated it from the top so they wouldn't get lost in it. The pyramid was also too exposed, so I planted *Anubias* to cover it without blocking the light. In the photo the pyramid is almost entirely covered.

The fish seem to like it. A few have paired off and now there are some young.

One day an aquarist came to visit me and saw this aquarium. He didn't like the fact that he couldn't tell whether there were any fish in there or not. I told him that that was a very human way of looking at it. We always put animals in cages so

RED ON GREEN

With two pieces of driftwood, a mound was constructed that slopes up toward the rear of the tank. This layout can be viewed from two directions. The CO_2 consumption is extremely high due to the fact that most of the plants are sunlight-loving plants (yousei-shokubutsu).

NO. 54 DATA

- ■ PHOTOGRAPHING : APRIL 1991
- ■ WATER TANK : W1200XD1000XH750(mm)
- ■ CONTENT : 900 liters
- ■ MAINTENANCE
- ● LIGHTING : 20WX20(400W)
- ● FILTERING : ORIGINAL POWER FILTER
- ● SUBSTRATE : OISO SAND
- ● CO_2 SUPPLY : ONCE EVERY ONE SECOND
- ● FERTILIZATION : 0.2cc/liter
- ● WATER CHANGE : ONCE A WEEK, 1/3 TANK OF WATER
- ■ WATER CONDITION
- ● TEMPERATURE : 25°C
- ● pH VALUE : 7.0
- ● TOTAL HARDNESS (GH) : 2°dH
- ● CARBONATE HARDNESS (KH) : 2°dH
- ● NITRITE (NO_2) : 0.1mg/liter
- ● NITRATE (NO_3) : LESS THAN 10mg/liter
- ● CO_2 : 21mg/liter
- ● O_2 : 9mg/liter

a large tank that will be viewed from two
tions, use two pieces of driftwood to support the
for a mound in a dynamic layout.

(3) Between the driftwood and the temple plant, plant
some *Anubias nana* so that it covers the "hairline" of the
long-stemmed plants, the place where they come out of
the sand.

(4) Sometimes it is better to leave most of the driftwood
in the open, and other times it is better to hide a lot of it.
In this layout, we're going to cover up quite a bit.

ice long-stemmed plants will be the focus, start
ig them from the top while considering the flow
plor schemata.

(5) It is easier to create a flowing layout of plants if you
start planting the long-stemmed plants from the back
and sides toward the center.

(6) Planting a line of *Anubias nana* through the center,
and red water lily between the foreground plants, helps
to bring the whole layout together.

The foundation of a layout that will be viewed from
directions is a harmonious balance between the
se of the sand and the flowing line of the driftwood.

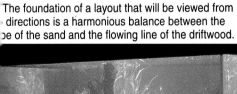

THE PRIMAL FOREST
This is a fine example of a centered layout, where driftwood and plants are placed in the center and surrounded by open space. This design is a must for the heckel discus, which swims laps around aquaria more than most fishes.

WELCOME TO THE JUNGLE, HECKEL DISCUS

No matter what fishes they are going to keep, most aquarists want their aquaria to look like jungles. I know that I strive for a lush, wildly overgrown look, though it is impossible to keep some fishes in that kind of enviroment. Large fishes like the pacu, and any other plant-eating fishes come to mind. But if it's possible, I attempt it. The discus, especially the Heckel discus, may be the most difficult to raise successfully in a jungle aquarium, success being defined as survival over a year.

Temperature is one problem: Heckel discus like it warmer than the plants do, around 30°C. Next, Heckel discus prefer around pH 5, while the plants want less acidity, around pH 6.5-7. Even lighting presents difficulties. Most plants need direct light and lots of it, but Heckel discus lurk in the shadows. These fundamental problems are enough to make one give up, but then there are some important rules to keep in mind. One is the old, "If the plants are healthy, the fish will be healthy." And this little bit of common sense: there must be some plants that grow in the Heckel discus' natural habitat. What follows is what I recorded in my notebook in the process of creating this aquarium.

Heckel discus require high temperatures and acidity, so plants can't be raised. But which is more adaptive, Heckel discus or the plants? Definitely Heckel discus. If the water quality is optimal then a little higher pH shouldn't kill it. And I have to try out lower temperatures at first, since the plants surely won't stand higher ones, and see what happens.

Use only tough plants: *Microsorium*, *Echinodorus tenellus*, willow moss, and Kurinam aquatica. The tank is 1200x1000x750mm and made of acrylic. Starting temperature. at 26°C, lighting with 10 PGIII 20W bulbs. To prevent pollution, frozen bloodworms are fed only once per day with a colander-type tool. Discharge CO_2 with a Fluval II day and night.

Now I have had this aquarium for two years and it's still healthy. The Heckel discus have nearly doubled in size and are showing beautiful colors. Pros will especially appreciate this subdued but fascinating aquarium that proves that Heckel discus can live in the jungle.

THE LITTLE PICTURE

The hobby I devote the most time to is photography, especially landscapes. I like taking landscape photos, and looking at other people's works. There is a big stack of collections by my bed, and I open one almost every night. From Hokkaido in the north to the islands of Okinawa in the south, I have a photographic memory of most famous landscapes.

One thing I like in landscape photography is a local photographer who knows the best season and time of day for shooting. Sometimes I visit a place and the landscape is so inferior to the photograph that inspired me to go there that I wonder if I'm in the right place. So I usually stay home with the photographic collections.

I also think it's interesting to compare different photographers' shots of the same landscape. Their viewpoints are always different. But shots by amateurs of the same place always look the same.

Now I like to take shots of isolated sections of nature, even different parts of the same landscape. A single lily on a cliff, or some unknown flower blooming by the roadside. I especially like sections of grass patches. There are all kinds of grass patches, from lush, tropical patches to patches of weeds in city lots. If you observe these closely, you realize that although they look messy and haphazard, the growth is actually very orderly and follows certain rules.

Sometimes you have to look at the little picture in order to better understand the big picture.

TO THE ETERNAL ONES

The great variety of plants in this very large aquarium have grown only more beautiful over the five years of its existence. I considered this to be my greatest work when I finished it, and it is still very special to me.

NO. 56 DATA

- ■ PHOTOGRAPHING : OCTOBER 1985
- ■ WATER TANK : W1800XD1000XH800(mm)
- ■ CONTENT : 1440 liters
- ■ MAINTENANCE
- ● LIGHTING : 40WX8(320W)
- ● FILTERING : POWER FILTER(X2)
- ● SUBSTRATE : OISO SAND
- ● CO_2 SUPPLY : ONCE EVERY ONE SECOND
- ● FERTILIZATION : 0.1cc/liter
- ● WATER CHANGE : ONCE EVERY TEN DAYS,
  1/3 TANK OF WATER
- ■ WATER CONDITION
- ● TEMPERATURE : 26℃
- ● pH VALUE : 6.8
- ● TOTAL HARDNESS (GH) : 2°dH
- ● CARBONATE HARDNESS (KH) : 2°dH
- ● NITRITE (NO_2) : 0.1mg/liter
- ● NITRATE (NO_3) : LESS THAN 10mg/liter
- ● CO_2 : 15mg/liter
- ● O_2 : 6mg/liter

ARTIFICE OVER NATURE

 In autumn, the distinguished professor from Kyoto University and authority on animal ecology Dr. Kawanabe comes to Niigata University to lecture. For the past ten years or so, professor Kawanabe has visited my home, and we always have wonderful talks in which he explains ecology to me in plain and simple terms. He is much easier to understand than a scholarly book, and much nicer to have around. One of his specialties is Lake Tanganyika, which is located between Zaire and Tanzania, and is the home of several popular species of dwarf cichlids, fishes of great interest to me.
 Of course, it was an aquarium that provided the opportunity for us to meet. I asked him if he would tell me what he thought of the aquarium in the photo. It was that depressing time of year when the leaves have mostly fallen and the trees look dead, but that's also the time when aquaria look best.
 When he first saw it, he was impressed and asked if it would be difficult to install one in his research lab. I was at a loss as to how to reply. Professor Kawanabe is the leading ecologist in the country. I didn't want to presume to explain things to such a great man.
 I told him that he could keep an aquarium like this in his lab if he copied this layout and closely monitored the water conditions. But when I had set it up four years before, I anticipated how it would develop many years later, and this kind of intuition, which had led to such a beautiful result, required a lot of experience.
 He nodded and said something that impressed me a great deal.
 "Yes, such a beautiful waterscape doesn't exist in nature. Only artifice made by human hands can attain this beauty."

TOUCHES OF COLOR

The composition of driftwood covered with *Microsorium* on the sides leaves enough space for the wild discus. This is the first aquarium that green discus has spawned in.

NO. 57 DATA

■ PHOTOGRAPHING : OCTOBER 1986
■ WATER TANK : W1800XD1000XH800(mm)
■ CONTENT : 1440 liters
■ MAINTENANCE
● LIGHTING : 40WX8(320W)
● FILTERING : POWER FILTER(X2)
● SUBSTRATE : SEA SAND
● CO_2 SUPPLY : ONCE EVERY THREE SECONDS
● FERTILIZATION : UNNECESSARY
● WATER CHANGE : ONCE A WEEK, 1/2 TANK OF WATER
■ WATER CONDITION
● TEMPERATURE : 27°C
● pH VALUE : 6.8

● TOTAL HARDNESS (GH) : 3°dH
● CARBONATE HARDNESS (KH) : 3°dH
● NITRITE (NO_2) : 0.1mg/liter
● NITRATE (NO_3) : LESS THAN 20mg/liter
● CO_2 : 15mg/liter
● O_2 : 5mg/liter

HEALTHY PLANTS, HEALTHY FISHES

This is an old story, from back when my friend T. and I were traveling around on steam-engine trains collecting fishes. I can remember the sloshing sound of the plastic bags of water holding the fishes against the background chugging of the train. In those days, every tropical fish store had its showpiece aquarium, which contained the fishes that were too good to sell, like silver arowana or angelfish swimming through forests of Amazon sword plants. These aquaria were my first inspiration.

The one that held me spellbound was a 120x45x45cm aquarium with families of brown discus swimming through huge Amazon sword plants that must have had a hundred leaves. Even though those discus were a basic brown, I still think they could stand up to the color-improved breeds of today.

The owner of that store was an old man who would kindly talk to us. He was the first to teach me that healthy plants made for healthy fishes. And the proof of his words filled his store. The guppies in the water sprite and *Nitella*, the angels in the Amazon sword plants, the characins in the *Hygrophila* and *Vallisneria*, and those wonderful brown discus all had a vitality that outshone mere color. I learned early that gaudiness cannot compare to health in fishes.

DANCING IN THE LIGHT

This layout was designed for the turquoise discus. The highlight of this composition is the contrast between the clay-red base sand, the green *Anubias barteri*, and the blue of the discus.

NO. 58 DATA

- ■ PHOTOGRAPHING : NOVEMBER 1990
- ■ WATER TANK : W1800XD1000XH800(mm)
- ■ CONTENT : 1440 liters
- ■ MAINTENANCE
- ● LIGHTING : 40WX8(320W)
- ● FILTERING : ORIGINAL POWER FILTER
- ● SUBSTRATE : AKADAMA CERAMICS
- ● CO_2 SUPPLY : ONCE EVERY TWO SECONDS
- ● FERTILIZATION : UNNECESSARY
- ● WATER CHANGE : ONCE A WEEK, 1/2 TANK
  OF WATER
- ■ WATER CONDITION
- ● TEMPERATURE : 27°C
- ● pH VALUE : 6.9
- ● TOTAL HARDNESS (GH) : 3°dH
- ● CARBONATE HARDNESS (KH) : 3°dH
- ● NITRITE (NO_2) : 0.1mg/liter
- ● NITRATE (NO_3) : LESS THAN 20mg/liter
- ● CO_2 : 16mg/liter
- ● O_2 : 5mg/liter

MATSUKAWAYA AND THE BLUE DISCUS

In Tokyo, there is a discus specialty shop called Matsukawaya that is owned by a professional breeder and old friend of mine named Koryo Abe. He and my elder brother became friends because they both loved goldfish. My brother lived near his store, and when he came back to visit us in Niigata, he would always bring tales of the incredible fishes he saw there.

I was able to meet Mr. Abe in my last year of junior high school, and he taught me many interesting things about discus as we sat in front of a beautiful aquarium with blue discus among thriving lace plants. He told me that there was a one-in-a-million specimen that lived in the Amazon with blue lines running the length of its body, and with that fish he could breed something no one has ever seen before: an entirely blue discus.

Later I told my brother about what Mr. Abe had said, but he thought that although Mr. Abe was nice enough, he liked to exaggerate.

"An all-blue discus is impossible," he said.

Twenty years later, the turquoise discus was bred in the West. My friend Mr. Abe and I still talk about discus whenever we get together for drinks, and whenever the turquoise discus comes up, he smiles bitterly. He tells me that I swore I would raise an all-blue discus in a plant-filled aquarium one day, but I honestly don't recall ever saying it.

137

HILL BETWEEN WOODS

This is a good example of a V-shaped layout. The dense woods on the sides and the spacious hill covered with cryptocorynes in the center are graded in three steps. The key to this kind of composition is to maintain a smooth line from level to level. Characins are gathering on the hill.

NO. 59 DATA

- ■ PHOTOGRAPHING : DECEMBER 1991
- ■ WATER TANK : W1800XD1000XH800(mm)
- ■ CONTENT : 1440 liters
- ■ MAINTENANCE
- ● LIGHTING : 40WX5.20WX5(TOTAL 300W)
- ● FILTERING : ORIGINAL POWER FILTER
- ● SUBSTRATE : OISO SAND
- ● CO_2 SUPPLY : IC. CONTROLLER
- ● FERTILIZATION : 0.2cc/liter
- ● WATER CHANGE : ONCE EVERY TEN DAYS, 1/3 TANK OF WATER
- ■ WATER CONDITION
- ● TEMPERATURE : 26°C
- ● pH VALUE : 6.8
- ● TOTAL HARDNESS (GH) : 3°dH
- ● CARBONATE HARDNESS (KH) : 3°dH
- ● NITRITE (NO_2) : 0.1mg/liter
- ● NITRATE (NO_3) : LESS THAN 10mg/liter
- ● CO_2 : 14mg/liter
- ● O_2 : 6mg/liter

WHAT GOES 'ROUND, COMES 'ROUND

Violets bloom, then dandelions bloom. Every year spring comes with an exactness we forget in our spring fevers. The wildflowers in the snow country of Yamano all bloom at once as the snow melts. Except for the popular hepatica and ebine, the number of flowers hasn't changed much in the past ten years. The same goes for the birds and insects. The mountainous areas are so remote, they may as well be unofficial preserves. Unfortunately, the same cannot be said for the plains. Where only five years ago my children and I caught killifishes and frogs, now we find stinking creeks.

Seven years ago I kept a large fish, and regularly went to the stream behind my house for food. I would cast a net and come up with loach, crucian carp, bitterling, and moroco. In those days there were abundant frogs, too. However, though I caught a relatively small amount for a while, eventually I wasn't catching anything. The wildlife was gone.

One main cause of the destruction of the stream is the residential run-off from upstream that contains detergents. It is ironic that today people live so cleanly that their cleanliness is the source of terrible pollution.

A second factor is the crop dusting that affects the whole farming region. It used to be that chemicals were spread on the fields carefully, so as not to waste any of the expensive herbicides, pesticides, or fertilizers. Not any more. Now the noisy helicopters simply cover the whole area. Many places have laws banning the spreading of chemicals near surrounding towns, but this isn't the case where I live. One dusting day I numbly walked down a farm road that was covered with earthworms coming out of the ground to die.

It's like the Persian Gulf War, daily bombings of chemicals and the only refuge, the middle of the water, flooded with poisonous detergent gas. The mass media point to the development of resorts and golf courses in pristine enviroments, but the enviromental destruction most people don't know about is taking place in the farming areas.

We are all indirectly threatened. It cannot be healthy to eat rice grown in land that frogs cannot survive on. We, at the top of the food chain, must remember: what goes 'round, comes 'round.

A mizuoobako (*Omzia*) flowers in a marsh.

140

OLD GROWTH FOREST

This is the greatest example of an aquarium that imitates nature in order to surpass it. This three ton aquarium is in great health.

NO. 60 DATA

- ■ PHOTOGRAPHING : OCTOBER 1991
- ■ WATER TANK : W1800XD1800XH900(mm)
- ■ CONTENT : 2900 liters
- ■ MAINTENANCE
- ● LIGHTING : 40WX10(400W)
- ● FILTERING : ORIGINAL POWER FILTER
- ● SUBSTRATE : OISO SAND
- ● CO_2 SUPPLY : ONCE EVERY ONE SECOND
- ● FERTILIZATION : UNNECESSARY
- ● WATER CHANGE : ONCE EVERY TWO WEEKS, 1/3 TANK OF WATER
- ■ WATER CONDITION
- ● TEMPERATURE : 26°C
- ● pH VALUE : 6.9
- ● TOTAL HARDNESS (GH) : 2°dH
- ● CARBONATE HARDNESS (KH) : 1°dH
- ● NITRITE (NO_2) : 0.1mg/liter
- ● NITRATE (NO_3) : LESS THAN 10mg/liter
- ● CO_2 : 15mg/liter
- ● O_2 : 6mg/liter

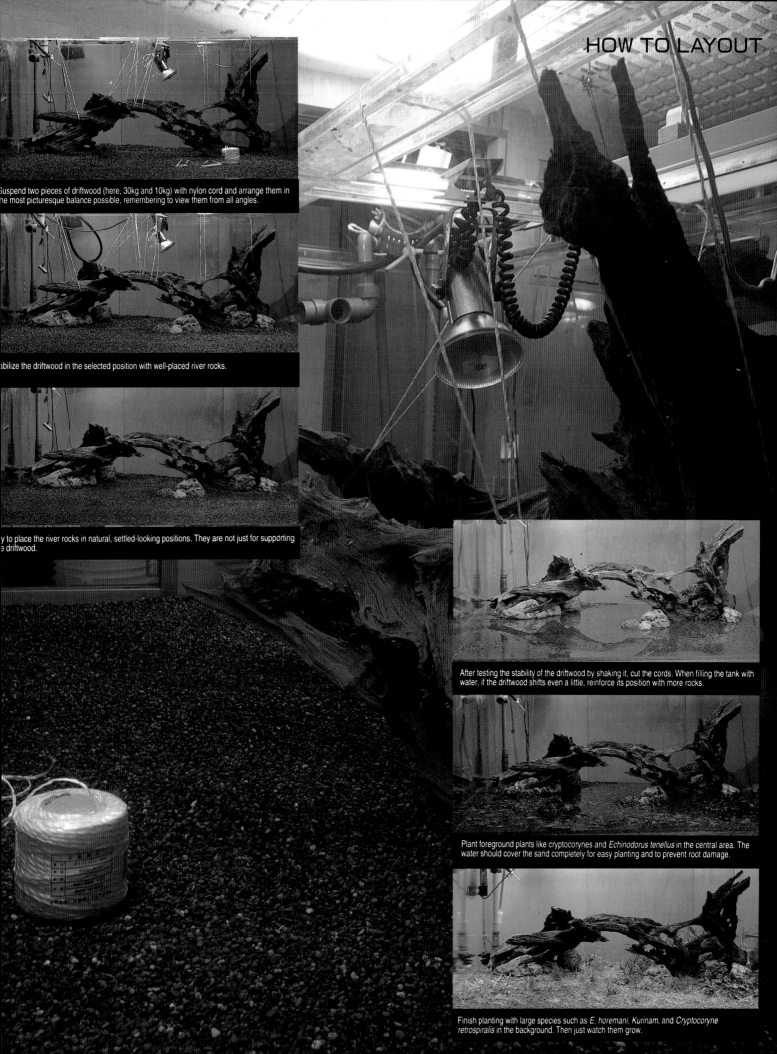

Suspend two pieces of driftwood (here, 30kg and 10kg) with nylon cord and arrange them in the most picturesque balance possible, remembering to view them from all angles.

...abilize the driftwood in the selected position with well-placed river rocks.

...y to place the river rocks in natural, settled-looking positions. They are not just for supporting ...e driftwood.

After testing the stability of the driftwood by shaking it, cut the cords. When filling the tank with water, if the driftwood shifts even a little, reinforce its position with more rocks.

Plant foreground plants like cryptocorynes and *Echinodorus tenellus* in the central area. The water should cover the sand completely for easy planting and to prevent root damage.

Finish planting with large species such as *E. horemani*, *Kurinam*, and *Cryptocoryne retrospiralis* in the background. Then just watch them grow.

Views of one of my tanks.

THE COLORFUL ENCYCLOPEDIA OF FISHES

When I was a child we used wood fires to cook and heat the bath. This is still not uncommon in mountain villages. Since we lived on a farming plain, we had to go to the nearest mountain village every year to buy firewood, and that was one of my mother's jobs. She used to take me along, and I would ride in the empty cart she pulled, and help her haul the load back home.

One day, while bringing a load of wood, she told me she would buy me something for my help. I immediately asked for the *Colorful Encyclopedia of Plants*. But when we got to the bookstore, all they had was the *Colorful Encyclopedia of Fishes*, which I accepted with some disappointment. Looking back, that bit of chance had a great impact on my life.

This was the first book I ever owned. I remember the beautiful illustrations well, though I no longer have the book. Every night I opened it before bed and tried to memorize the name of one fish. I learned that the

scientific name for the coelacanth, *Latimeria chalumnae*, comes from Ms. Latimer, the great scientist who studied it, and the Chalumna River, near where it was caught in South Africa. I memorized all kinds of facts the way other kids memorize batting averages and RBI's. I started to buy other fish books with my allowance, and when I got tired of fishes, I read all of Fabre's *Souvenirs entomologiques* and Seton's *Wild Animals I Have Known*.

Now I'm in the grown-up business of producing aquaria, but every time I start a new work I think of a story. Even a piece of driftwood has a story, the story of its life as a growing tree, its death, the many days it was slapped smooth by rain and wind, and the forces that brought it into my hands. I can thank my mother for the first book that led a boy who hated school to other books, and to a life of imagination.

DEEP GREEN GLOW

The plants and open spaces of this layout were designed for raising the altum-angelfish. The dense growth resembles their native habitat, and this makes them more beautiful.

NO. 61 DATA

- ■ PHOTOGRAPHING : JANUARY 1990
- ■ WATER TANK : W1800XD1600XH900(mm)
- ■ CONTENT : 2590 liters
- ■ MAINTENANCE
- ● LIGHTING : 40WX9(360W)
- ● FILTERING : ORIGINAL POWER FILTER
- ● SUBSTRATE : AKADAMA CERAMICS
- ● CO_2 SUPPLY : ONCE EVERY ONE SECOND
- ● FERTILIZATION : 0.1cc/liter
- ● WATER CHANGE : ONCE EVERY TEN DAYS, 1/3 TANK OF WATER
- ■ WATER CONDITION
- ● TEMPERATURE : 26°C
- ● pH VALUE : 6.8
- ● TOTAL HARDNESS (GH) : 2°dH
- ● CARBONATE HARDNESS (KH) : 2°dH
- ● NITRITE (NO_2) : 0.1mg/liter
- ● NITRATE (NO_3) : LESS THAN 20mg/liter
- ● CO_2 : 19mg/liter
- ● O_2 : 8mg/liter

THE RISE AND FALL OF *ANABAS*

For some reason, snails always seem to appear in plant aquaria. They must be mixed in with the plants beforehand. Sometimes the population explodes and is a real problem. Once a long time ago I had an aquarium filled with red ramshorn snails, which were quite pretty, but usually it's the dull, ugly snails that multiply in the aquarium. Many tropical fishes eat snails, such as the gouramis, the freshwater puffers, and the cichlids, like angelfish and *Anomalochromis thomasi*. So now I put a dwarf shimegaeru (frog) in from the beginning as a snail eater. It is one of the essential tank cleaners, along with *Otocinclus* for brown algae, and yamato-numaebi (shrimp) for filamentous algae.

The fish and shime gaeru (frog) are able to eat average snails, but it seems that the only thing that can handle the big ones is the *Anabas* (kinoboriou), a relative of the gouramis. These find large snails as soon as they move and gobble them right up. So one day I put five of them into a big aquarium, and within a week all of the snails were gone. However, soon the *Anabas* were terrorizing the tank. They chased the other fishes and injured them. They hogged all the food. They even uprooted plants!

My patience ran out and I decided to evict the nuisances. First I tried to lure them into a container with bloodworms—but they saw through my plan. Next I tried a method that had worked before with

angelfish. I waited until night when the tank was dark and the fish were asleep, then I clicked on a flashlight and tried to grab them. But their reactions were too quick and in a flash they were hiding in the plants. I decided to try hooking them, and bought a fishing kit and baited the hook with krill. But the *Anabas*'s mouth was bigger than I thought and I couldn't catch it. So I went back to the store to see what they recommended.

"Just what are you trying to catch?"

"A 7cm. tropical fish called *Anabas*."

"Oh, you're going overseas?" they asked with interest.

"No, no, it's in an aquarium in my home," I answered. They laughed.

"In that case, you should get a net at a goldfish shop. They can help you out."

"No, those are no good."

"What do you mean, they're no good?" They were starting to sound annoyed.

I told them about my aquarium, how it was ten times bigger than the family bath, nearly 2 meters long and 2.5 tons, and was full of plant life. They helped me out, then. It took a while, but later that day, human ingenuity finally outsmarted the *Anabas* and they were caught.

149

A DRAGONFLY IN WINTER

Sometimes I find dragonfly nymphs (yago) living in an aquarium, most likely brought in on some of the plants. They seem to be able to survive only in large, thriving tanks. It probably has something to do with the food supply.

One room of my home has been converted to a greenhouse in which I keep tropical fishes, frogs, and so on. In the winter, though, we also hang our laundry in it, and on cold mornings that's where I get dressed.

In that room there is a large aquarium (240x60x60cm) in which a yago had been living since the fall. There were no larger fishes, which are its natural enemies, so it was living rather freely in there. Then suddenly we stopped seeing it and forgot about it.

One unforgettably harsh winter morning in January, the wind was howling and whipping snow outside as I hurried into the greenhouse in my pajamas with my clothes under my arm. As I started to dress, I heard a funny buzz go by my head. I continued to put on my clothes and heard it again from the other direction. Then I saw the strangest dragonfly I have ever seen. It was tortoise-shell colored! It must have been mixed in with the African plants I'd bought. I went and awakened my wife and kids to see this incredible sight. I called my parents and told them. Then I told my friends about it, and we seized the excuse to have a party. We are a strange bunch.

Unfortunately, for lack of mosquito food it lived only three days. We couldn't let it outside in the dead of winter. Bad as I felt, there was nothing to do but watch it die. Since then, many Japanese dragonflies have grown up in our aquaria, but never a tortoise-shell colored one like the winter dragonfly.

O U  T

THE BASIC CONCEPTS OF AQUATIC PLANT LAYOUT

As in all creative work, there is a strong element of taste involved in aquatic plant layout, so it is difficult to simply say, "This is the best way." But no matter how artistically a layout is designed, if the plants aren't healthy or the tank is choked with algae, it won't be much to look at. Conversely, even an awkward design will have some appeal if the aquarium is in good shape. The *sine qua non* of all good layouts is the good condition of the plants.

Now, there are two basic types of aquatic plant layouts. One is modeled on gardens, and the other is modeled on nature. The first type can also be called the Dutch style, and imitates the orderliness of a flowerbed which is organized by flower size and color. Long-stemmed plants are used often, and the look is luxurious and bright. A tulip garden is a typical example of this style.

The natural style is harder to pin down, because different people focus on different aspects of nature. The one thing all the techniques that fall under this heading have in common is that they were learned through observing plants in their natural state.

There is, however, a fundamental idea that these two styles share, and that is the love and care of the aquarist, which is visible in the final product. Aquatic plant layout contests have become popular lately, and the quality of the work is steadily rising. The best ones always manage to express something about the individual spirit of the creator.

Perhaps the best way to improve one's work is to be exposed regularly to a wide variety of influences: landscapes, Japanese gardens, paintings, photographs, music. The Japanese people have been blessed with a land of great natural beauty. Our bow-shaped Japan stretches through many different climates and encompasses many different types of geography. Japanese have a long and distinguished tradition of extracting the beauty of nature for use in the arts and in daily life. This tradition is a diamond mine for aquarists, if they will only look.

Another very important quality of good aquarists is flexibility. If there isn't enough time for the work, or inspiration doesn't come, the artist doesn't force it, but waits for the right moment. The same goes for finances: if the desired tank seems too expensive, settle for a cheaper one. Then there will be enough money for accessories later. The aquarist needs leeway in time, money, and spirit. Nothing should be rushed or feel forced. I'm talking about the leisure to create.

Nature comes to look different when leisure time is set aside for it. When you are rushing to work, rain is a nuisance. When you have the time to observe little details, an empty city lot is full of magic. The power of observation is also important. How much do you notice? How much do you remember of what you see in nature? The details you notice and remember will greatly influence any form of expression, whether it is painting, photography, or aquarium layout.

THE COMPOSITION OF THE WATERSCAPE

When you come to "Composition" in an art textbook, there are a lot of confusing geometric figures and values that frighten off many people. But composition is not so difficult to understand. Everywhere around us are carefully designed compositions, from cigarette packages to postcards to magazine covers, and they are all designed to please the human eye. To do so, most rely on a simple ratio called the "golden section."

For example, we want to place a river rock in a 120cm tank. Most people wouldn't put it right in the center. They would place it somewhat to the right or left, and this is paradoxically more balanced, more appealing to our esthetic sensibility. The very best position, in the sense that people perceive it as the most balanced, has been known since antiquity. This ratio of 1:1.618 is the "golden section." This is the ratio where if there are two sections of a line, the smaller is to the larger as the larger is to the sum of the two. It can also be thought of as roughly 3/5.

People who are experienced in design don't even need to think about the golden section. It just comes naturally to them. Of course, it is also a good idea to deviate from the golden section and experiment with ratios that seem unbalanced, thereby injecting tension into the composition. Americans refer to the "golden section" as the *optical center*.

156

THE BASIC COMPOSITIONAL SHAPES

 In painting, architecture, photography, and all of the
arts, the use of space is of prime importance. Space
exists and serves important purposes in the arts just as
it does in nature, even in the densest forest. Depending
on ecological and meteorological conditions, these
spaces can be very beautiful. But aquarists have to
make their own conditions.

THE TRIANGULAR LAYOUT

 All types of triangles–equilateral, scalene, isosceles and irregular–can and should be used in
layouts. Triangles can be used in constructing the layout of the plants, the driftwood and rocks, and
the sand, and all the different directions they can be viewed from must be kept in mind.
 When we consider this fact, that it can be viewed from different sides, we realize that the aquarium
itself is a relatively new and complex art form.
 For the basic triangular layout, divide the side of the aquarium with a diagonal line so that there are
two triangles. The sand base slopes upward, so it is more shallow in front, gradually deepening
toward the rear. When viewed from the sides, the lower front section of the bottom triangle is
composed of short plants, and the higher rear section of tall ones. The increasing height of the
plants makes the diagonal line of the triangles.

THE MOUND-SHAPED COMPOSITION

The mound-shaped layout is made by placing driftwood, rocks, and tall plants in the center of the aquarium and leaving a circular space around the perimeter. This is a deceptively simple composition which actually requires great technique. A better balance is attained by placing the driftwood and rocks slightly off the tank's center. Tall tanks are best suited to this layout, and I have also used it in many tanks sized 60x45x30cm, 90x60x45cm, and 120x60x45cm.

THE U-SHAPED COMPOSITION

This is the mirror image of the mound-shaped composition. Driftwood, rocks, and tall plants are placed on the sides and space is left open in the center. The two sides should not be the same size, but rather in a 2:1, 3:1, or golden section ratio. This layout is well-suited to relatively long tanks (eg., 180x60x60cm), and is the easiest of the basic layouts. It is also the most common one in this book.

流木の配し方

自然の小川や渓流をよく観察すると、小さな流れの中にも様々なドラマが生まれていることが分かる。渓流の傍らには朽ちかけた流木がいくつもころがっており、苔やシダなどが活着し、長い歳月流木がそこに存在したことを物語っている。そしてまた、膨大な時間とドラマを推測し、どのような生の時代があって、どのようにしてここに流れついてきたのか考えると興味深い。水草レイアウトには、水質の悪化を招くので朽ちたものは使用できないが、このようなドラマを感じながらレイアウトに利用すると、水草の選定も全体の構成も意外にスムーズにいき、レイアウト作りもまた数倍楽しいものになる。

流木を使用する場合、専用に市販されているフィリピン産やアフリカ産のものなどは比重も重く堅いので、そのまま水槽に入れても浮いたり腐ったりすることはないが、日本産の流木はダムや湖底に相当長く沈んで堅い芯だけが残ったものでないと、暖かい熱帯魚水槽に沈めたとたん腐りだしてしまうものが多いので注意を要する。

外国産であっても、最初の頃は流木のアクが水中にゆっくり解け出してくる。これを放って置くと水は薄茶色になり、やがてコーヒー色に変わっていく。ここまでアクが出るのは相当の長時間水を取り替えない場合のことだが、普通の換水量を週1回励行していれば水の色が気になったりアクが水草に直接害を及ぼすことはない。むしろセット初期のバクテリアが少ない時は換水の量（回数）を増やすべきで、流木によって水が薄く色づいてきたら水を取り替える時期が来たという警告につながるので、逆に便利だと思っている。アクがどうしても気になる場合は、古いナベなどで煮沸すると出にくくなる。

流木の形

水草レイアウト用に使用する流木は様々で、1つ1つ形が異なっている。流木を選定する基準はないが、レイアウトする水槽の大きさに比例したものを選ぶこ

とが大切である。水槽に比べて大きすぎる流木は圧迫感があり、見ていて息苦しい。できれば自分のイメージした水景の流木よりひと回り小さめのものを選んだ方が、水草の植栽をする上でもやりやすくなる。また形の複雑なものは、流木のイメージが強すぎて水草が貧弱に感じられることもあるので気をつけたい。

水草のレイアウトをする場合、気に入った流木を購入した後で水草を選定しレイアウトしていく方法と、先に述べた凸凹△方式の構成をあらかじめ決めておき、その構図に適した流木を使用する方法がある。前者は比較的初心者に多く、後者はベテランのレイアウターに多い。また流木の形を見て構図を決める方法もあるが、これは前述の両方をうまく利用しており、現実には中堅級のレイアウターに多い。

実際にレイアウトされた流木を見ると、水槽の壁面に立てかけたりオーバーハングするように配されたものは動的な迫力がある。ただ、この方法は空間を水槽の後方にとらないと圧迫感も生まれてくる。また、

空間に向かって左右の流木が伸び出すレイアウト
は□形形式の代表的な配し方で、ここにシダなどを
□させると全体に立体感のある水景になる。
□くて重心がしっかりした（たとえば切り株のよう
□形状を持つ流木は、出来るだけ安定感のあるも
□選び周りの空間に対比させることによって動的
□力と静的安定感を演出したい。あまり形状が複
□ない横長の流木は、三角形の構図を作るための
□高架用の土止めにしたり、ゆるやかな底床に置
□流動的なリズムを演出するために使用する。この
□流木は、主役として水草の良さを100％引き出し
□時に利用できる。

POSITIONING DRIFTWOOD

Decaying parts of trees are easy to find in rivers that run through wooded areas, and these pieces of driftwood convey a sense of nature's time scale, the long cycle of life-death-rebirth of which we only glimpse fragments. Rotting wood is bad for water quality, but any good piece of driftwood evokes a sense of non-human time. In fact, dry driftwood, with its fossilized look, may give this impression even more strongly. In any case, this quality can be an inspiration during layout.

Fine driftwood from the Philippines and Africa can be bought in specialty shops. These are dense and hard, and there is no danger of their floating or rotting in the aquarium. As for local specimens, the only safe ones are pieces that have been submerged a long time, and of which only the hard core remains. Otherwise, exercise caution, since wood often will begin to rot once it is placed in a warm tropical fish tank.

The wood may leak tannic acid and turn the water a coffee-colored brown, but if the tank is regularly changed (once a week), there shouldn't be a problem. In fact, it may be helpful, since in the early stages, when there is little bacteria in the water, a brown tint serves as a convenient warning that the time to change the water has come. If the tannin is really a bother, boil the driftwood in an old pot, and it will be secreted much more slowly.

THE SHAPE OF THE DRIFTWOOD

Like every snowflake, every piece of driftwood is different. There are no set standards for choosing a piece, but the first aspect to consider is size. It may be best to select one slightly smaller than you imagined you would need, because driftwood that is too big for an aquarium takes over the whole waterscape and ruins it. One that is too complicated will also detract from the rest of the aquarium.

There are a few ways to plan with driftwood. First, select a piece that is appealing, put it in the tank, and then build the layout around it. This is the way beginners usually go. Another option is to choose a layout shape first, then set off searching for a piece that will make that layout work. Pros usually take this path. A sort of middle road is to pick out a nice piece, then try to plan the layout before actually taking it home.

The driftwood should be placed so that it leans against the wall of the aquarium or has many overhanging branches jutting out. This gives it a more dynamic quality than one just lying there. It is even more effective if space behind the driftwood is left open to highlight it.

Another way to add vitality is to plant ferns on the driftwood. This is especially good when using one piece on each side of a U-shaped layout and both are stretching toward the center.

When using a large, centered piece like an old tree stump, choose a stable-looking one and focus on building tension by creating a dynamic composition around this quiet center.

Long, simple pieces make good supports for soil mounds in triangular layouts. Try to place them so as to highlight their flowing lines.

ROCK ARRANGEMENTS

Rocks can be classified for our purposes by where they are found, for example mountain rocks, river rocks, sea rocks, etc., or by their material name, such as granite, andesite, petrified wood, and so on. Most rocks can be used in aquaria, but rocks containing lime, such as limestone or sea rocks with shells mixed in, should be avoided because they will increase the pH and hardness of the water excessively.

While driftwood varies mainly in shape, rocks vary mainly in color. Black river rocks give the aquarium a cold feel, and brown petrified wood adds warmth to the layout. Too colorful rocks are abrasive and disturb the harmony of the aquarium. However, it is important to use a variety of sizes.

The largest rock is the centerpiece, and an easy way to attain balance is to place smaller rocks around it in

an irregular triangular arrangement. The centerpiece rock should be the most attractive one available in shape, size, color, and character, and the smaller rocks around it should resemble it in these aspects like younger siblings. When the rocks are of different types, the composition doesn't come together.

When choosing a rock, the important qualities are subtlety and composure. Every rock should be the strong and silent type.

Rock arrangements are best modeled on nature. Any walk along a river reveals dozens of interesting constructions. One can't go wrong imitating a famous Japanese rock garden, either. But designers of these have traditionally gone in search of models in rivers and waterfalls, sketched what they found, and based their work on their discoveries.

162

DRESSING UP ROCKS AND DRIFTWOOD

If rocks and driftwood are simply placed naked into the aquarium, they upset the balance by being too raw. They will look unnatural. They need to be dressed up with mosses or ferns so that they will fit in and have that aged, wabi-sabi look.

To attach willow moss (*Fontinalis*) or Java moss (*Vesicularia*) onto rocks or driftwood, place it on the surface that will be visible and secure it tightly with black cotton thread. The moss should not be so thick that it is difficult to attach. After one or two months, the thread rots off, and the moss will have taken to the surface and will continue to grow.

Another method is to insert the moss into cracks in the wood or rock with a pair of tweezers. The result should be the same but the procedure is more time-consuming.

For attaching onto driftwood ferns like *Microsorium* or plants like *Anubias* that put down roots, use those plastic ties that are used to secure trash bags. After one or two months, they should have extended roots into the wood. Carefully observe how much they have taken, and slowly remove the ties when it is safe.

To attach unattachable floating plants like the liverwort, *Riccia*, use a very thin fishing line (monofilament) to tie it securely, wrapping it around and around so that it's attached at many points along the rock or driftwood. It is important not to use a cord that can rot, because then the *Riccia* will come loose and float to the surface. Clear plastic fishing line can be good for reflecting more light onto the *Riccia*.

The *Riccia* may grow to such a size that its floating power is greater than the cord. Spreading some heavy sand on it should take care of this problem. After a long time, *Riccia* will lose its floating ability and remain submerged without restraints.

(1) *Microsorium* attached to driftwood with plastic ties.
(2) *Bolbitis* attached to driftwood with plastic ties.
(3) Willow moss being tied to driftwood with black cotton thread.
(4) *Riccia* tied to granite with monofilament.

③

④

AQUATIC PLANTS

The Dutch style of aquatic plant layout is based on the Western esthetic of ideal forms and symmetry, while the natural style intentionally upsets the balance of the composition and seeks harmony among disparate parts. As I have emphasized in this book, nature itself is the best model for this style. The orderly beauty that can be found in the chaos of nature if it is observed closely and carefully is amazing. It is the best teacher.

CREATING THE FOREGROUND (BOTTOM PLANTS)

After developing an eye for observing nature, one realizes that the most important plants in a miniature landscape are the short plants, which I call bottom plants. These make up the base and fill out the picture. Poor layouts are usually the result of either the aquarist not paying enough attention to the bottom plants, or an unnatural way of planting.

Some of the common plants chosen as bottom plants are *Echinodorus tenellus, Sagittaria subulata,* hair grass (*Eleocharis*), cobra grass, *Cryptocoryne minima, C. rubra,* and *C. nevillii.* In larger tanks, some species that grow somewhat taller can be used, such as *E. latifolius, E. grisebachii, Anubias nana,* and *C. wendti.* Finally, it is unusual, but *Riccia* and willow moss growing on rock or driftwood may be used as bottom plants.

USING PLANTS AS HIGHLIGHTS

A few well-placed, slightly taller plants in the foreground with interestingly shaped leaves, then some broad-leafed *Echinodorus* or *Anubias* in the middle and background, can lend the whole composition a sense of depth. These plants lead the eye along the waterscape.

Naturally, the size of the bottom plants will vary between a 60cm and a 180cm tank, but the types of plants used as highlights will also be different. For example, in a 60cm tank a very small plant like *Glossostigma* would be used for the bottom plant, and it could be highlighted with hair grass, which would be a bottom plant in a larger tank, in which case it would be highlighted in turn by a slightly larger plant.

The only general rule is not to use long-stemmed plants as highlights, unless it is like pearl grass, whose leaves develop near the base of the stem. Since *Cryptocoryne, Echinodorus, Kurinam,* and *Anubias* are all available in different sizes, they are very convenient for use as highlights.

MAKING THE BACKGROUND

The background finishes up the layout and defines its space. In contrast to the sparser foreground, the background is dense and gives the aquarium the appearance of wilderness.

Most often used in the background are long-stemmed plants, though there are exceptions such as *Vallisneria* and *Aponogeton.* There is a vast number of aquatic plants that can be used, but some of the most common species are pearl grass, *Mayaca, Alternanthera reineckii, Rotala macrantha, Rotala indica,* large-leaf *Hygrophila, Hygrophla polysperma, Ludwigia,* and the Dutch plant.

The greater the variety of plants in an aquarium, the more natural it looks. The ideal quantities range from about ten different leaf shapes and colors in a small tank, up to a hundred in a very large one.

Red-leaf plants are the flowers of the aquarium, so be sure the light and CO_2 needs of these plants are exactly met so that they can show their best colors. These must be used sparingly, however, so as not to overwhelm with color and destroy the quiet refinement with gaudiness.

Interestingly enough, like land plants, certain aquatic plants are compatible and others are not. For example, willow moss and *Microsorium* grow well together, but *Echinodorus tenellus* and *E. grisebachii* do not. If I ever write another book on aquatic plants, I would like to focus on plant compatibility.

TOOLS

 The necessary tools of the aquarist
used in layout and trimming are the
tweezers, scissors, and sand leveler. I
could not do my work without these.
Of course, all tweezers are not alike.
Surgical instruments and precision
machine tools are very expensive but
the quality matches the price.
Gardening and bonsai tools are more
affordable but none are made
specifically for aquatic plants and they
break more often. Sometimes, I find
that the cheapest tools of all work
best: my fingers.
 Good tweezers are sharp at the
point, meet perfectly, can be pinched
shut with the fingertips without much
effort, and are easy to use
underwater. Especially when the
tank's dimensions are 60cm or less,
tweezers are absolutely indispensable
to effective and attractive planting.
 Scissors must be sharp enough to
cut stems without crushing them. The
longer and thinner it is, the better for
trimming hard-to-reach places.
 There are no tools sold for leveling
sand, so I use the surgical instrument
in the photo. I use this for smoothing
out the sand and filling in holes made
after planting.
 The long spoon-like tool is used for
both planting and uprooting large
plants when tweezers or fingers alone
don't do the trick. I dig around the
plant with it as I push in or pull out
with the tweezers.

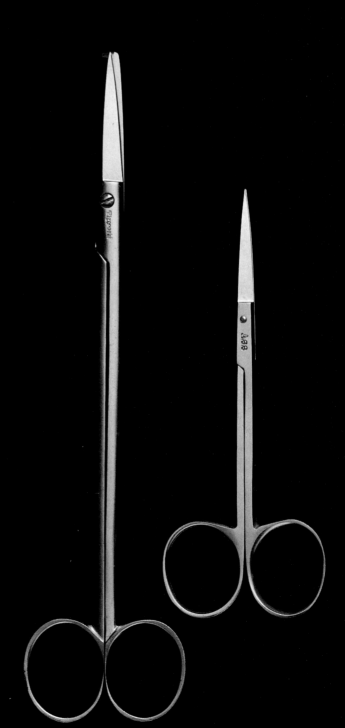

MATERIALS

In creating a waterscape that reproduces nature or is in the style of a Japanese garden, rock is the basic element, the rawest material. At present many different kinds of rocks are imported for use in gardening and aquaria, and some of the best are Malaysian and American petrified wood. Its pale coloring is even better than driftwood for bringing out the green of the plants.

When arranging rocks, don't worry about the individual characters as much as the look as a whole when 3 or 5 are put together. Some rocks need another rock to make them look right. The best way to go about finding the best arrangement is to actually try out as many as necessary. Put down the base sand and start arranging until the perfect combination appears.

Some rocks should be placed standing up, some lying down, and some leaning. It depends on their shape, and it takes experimentation to find the right way.

Finally, there are a few principles to keep in mind: don't line up rocks of the same shape or size; don't use differently colored rocks or rocks from different regions in the same layout; and don't use a rock in a way that contradicts its essence. That last one will take some experience.

WATER

P L A N T

HOW TO RAISE AQUATIC PLANTS

In this section I want to relate some technical know-how regarding the raising of healthy aquatic plants. There are major differences between raising land plants and aquatic plants, so throw away your preconceptions. A land plant can grow alone in a yard; it lives off water and the 0.03% of CO_2 in the air using solar power through photosynthesis. A fish aquarium is much simpler, too. Basically, just feed them and they're okay. But in a plant aquarium, the plants must coexist with fishes, and the natural processes that bring life-enabling substances to plants in the wild are all controlled artificially. Under such tightly-controlled conditions, there is little room for error.

CARBON DIOXIDE

Everyone knows that every green plant needs carbon dioxide (CO_2). Without it, they could not assimilate the nutrients they need to live. Plants get CO_2 from the air and from water. The CO_2 in water is mainly a product of bacteria breaking down organic matter. In the aquarium, the amount of CO_2 that fishes emit through respiration is limited and quickly used up by the plants. This causes the water to have a high pH (become

measuring the pH level. If the pH level falls below the neutral level of 7, then there is too much CO_2 in the water, and the water is acidic. If it rises above 7, then there is much too little CO_2, and the water is alkaline. The computerized pH controller operates on this principle, but it is important to remember that it is just a convenient relationship. Thinking that pH and CO_2 are the same thing could lead to trouble.

For example, if there is a large quantity of bacteria due to an old sand base or old filter material, the pH level will fall. This is caused by either the bacteria's respiration or the nitrate byproducts of its decomposition of ammonia. If the fall in pH is caused by bacterial respiration, it is good to increase the amount of CO_2. But if it is caused by an increase in nitrates, it is better to add more water to the aquarium.

Additional CO_2 has to be added for these reasons most often in the earlier stages of the aquarium. When there is a lot of bacteria in an older aquarium, sometimes the plants can live off just the CO_2 generated by the bacteria, as long as the species and number of plants is suitable.

To find out how much CO_2 the plants are consuming,

C O N C E

alkaline). Providing enough CO_2 to the ecosystem of the aquarium is a primary task of aquarists. The challenge is maintaining a natural balance between the requirements of the fishes and the plants.

Various devices are available now for providing CO_2 to plant aquaria. If the aquarium is a large one, a computerized controller is essential for avoiding chronic CO_2 shortages. Smaller aquaria don't need as much control. If the plants aren't growing, they either need more CO_2 or more light.

There is a simple way to tell if the plants are photosynthesizing or not. Observe the plants one or two hours after discharging the CO_2. There should be small bubbles forming on the leaves as a sign that photosynthesis is taking place. If not, and the amount of CO_2 has been increased, then the problem most likely has to do with the lighting or the filter.

The level of CO_2 in the water can be determined by

compare the pH levels of the morning and evening. The pH should be at its lowest level in the morning (before turning on the light) after a night of fishes respirating oxygen and expiring CO_2, and at its highest level in the evening (before lights out) after a day of plant absorption of CO_2 and discharge of oxygen. The greater the difference between these two values, the greater the consumption of CO_2, and therefore the greater the health of the plants.

In the daytime, if the pH level won't go down no matter how much CO_2 is added, it is because the plants are continually engaged in photosynthesis. The ideal pH level for aquatic plants is 6.8, but a value of around 7.5 during the day is not unusual and will not harm them. Rather, potential harm comes from using chemicals that force the pH level down. Potassium carbonate is often used to raise the pH level, but chemicals that lower it are to be avoided.

P   T   &   C   O₂

FILTERS

Filters, the purifiers of the aquarium's water, come in different forms and with different functions. Most common are the top filter, the bottom filter (undergravel), which uses the substrate sand as filter material, and the power filter, which is located outside the aquarium. The filter that is best for the plants will be the best for the whole aquarium. The plants release the oxygen that the animals need, and they have water-purifying powers. That is, the plants will absorb harmful substances like ammonia and nitrogen that the animals discharge. These are some of the reasons why I say, "healthy plants, healthy fish."

Let's consider filters from the standpoint of the three essential needs of plants: water, light, and carbon dioxide.

Aquatic plants depend on the water for life. The fine plants that aquarists raise, however, survive in a nutrient-poor environment. When the water becomes too rich in nutrients, lower plants (algae) begin to thrive and choke out the higher plants. Even the best filters available cannot keep the water pure enough to wipe out this possibility, so aquarists have to regularly change the water as a secondary purification measure.

If the filter is too small or too weak, no amount of water changing will prevent algae from invading the aquarium. Filters in poor condition also lead to more sickness among the fishes. The bacteria and microbes in healthy filters fight pathogens and algae, making it difficult for them to enter the

has some faults. First, substrate fertilizer cannot be used. Second, once the bottom sand ages it is no longer an efficient filter material, and third, as the plants grow their roots will interfere with the flow of water through the substrate. This method is actually effective in the early stages of the aquarium. It brings oxygenated water directly to the plants' roots and evens out the temperature difference between substrate and water. Though this improves growth in the early stages, in fact it only brings the aquarium closer to the problems that are sure to develop later. Of course, this doesn't apply to the aquarist who changes the layout frequently.

Filters can be further divided into physical filters and biological filters. Physical filters use activated charcoal or zeolite to remove ammonia and nitrogen from the water. The more common biological filters use microorganisms that nitrify ammonia and nitrogen, that is, change them into less harmful nitrates through oxidation. Both methods have their advantages, and in many plant aquaria, both are used simultaneously.

In the early stages, until the nitrobacteria have fully developed in the filter material, physical filtration with activated charcoal can be relied upon. But rather than using only the charcoal, putting a bottom layer of a rough, large granule filter material will not only catch large particles of waste but at the same time feed the nitrobacteria in

F I L

water.

Now, in regard to light, the top filter is potentially disadvantageous in that it will probably block some of the light that the plants need. In plant aquaria, the light must be totally unimpeded.

Finally, let's look at CO_2. Filters that aerate or churn up the water let CO_2 escape. It is like shaking up a can of soda. All the CO_2 goes hissing out into the air, and the soda is flat. Plants don't like flat soda anymore than we do. Air lift filters, pipe tube, shower, and other concentrated filters, and any filter that brings the water into direct contact with the air, causes the water to lose CO_2. Water can absorb 70 times more CO_2 than air can, but it also escapes much more easily. These filters are fine for aquaria that keep only fishes, but aquaria designed for plants cannot use filters that create CO_2-dispersing turbulence or allow direct contact between the water and air.

The filter that passes in all three areas is the one specially designed for raising aquatic plants: the self-contained power filter. But even a power filter cannot compensate for poor practices like shower-style draining that creates turbulence. The drainage tube must be located below the surface and not spray the water.

The power filter can be misused. The method of undergravel filtering with the discharge pulled up from below the substrate

preparation for 100% biological filtration. Activated charcoal loses its filtering ability in one or two weeks. But when that time comes, effective microorganisms will be flourishing on the charcoal.

Now, it is very important to understand the timing of the change from physical to biological filtration. The charcoal should not be immediately removed in order to convert to biological filtration, because the nitrobacteria on the rough lower layer will not be strong enough to carry the filtration burden of the entire aquarium alone, the balance will be immediately thrown off kilter, and fishes will begin to die and algae will sprout up. The bacteria in both areas have been filtering up to this point, so that is the amount that is needed. Therefore, the charcoal could continue to be used, but as the material for biological filtration.

One disadvantage of charcoal is that it is a very fine material that needs to be cleaned occasionally to prevent clogs. So it is usually replaced with a material that is just the right size and good for bacterial growth. There is no hard and fast rule for when to change materials, and judging the timing is difficult. Generally, the activated charcoal should be replaced at the time of the first or second clogging. Whether the charcoal is going to be cleaned or replaced, the bottom layer must not be cleaned until the whole filter is switched to biological filtration.

BIOLOGICAL FILTERS

It is no exaggeration to say that the condition of an aquarium depends on the performance of its biological filter. When the filter's microorganisms are functioning well, the water is crystal clear and there is no algal growth.

The chemical reaction that expresses the oxidation process carried out by the nitrobacteria which converts harmful ammonia into harmless nitrate is $NH_3. NO_2. NO_3.$ The bacteria that converts ammonia (NH_3) into nitrite (NO_2) is called *Nitrosomonas*, and the bacteria that converts that into nitrate (NO_3) is called *Nitrobactor*. It is said that the remaining nitrate is about 70 times less poisonous than the nitrite, but if enough accumulates in the water it can become harmful. Therefore, it is always necessary to change the water even when using a top-of-the-line filter. The filter that can completely dispose of nitrates hasn't been built.

To detemine the nitrate and nitrite levels of the water, there are both analog data meters and chemical reagents. The latter are much less expensive, if a little inconvenient. A good estimate of these nitrate levels can be made from the pH level as well. As the level of nitrates increases, the pH decreases, and water that is high in nitrites will have a high pH. If the pH hits 5.0, then it's likely that the nitrate level is high.

The pH is affected because of two things. The first is that nitrates are themselves acids. The second is that when nitrobacteria oxidize organic materials, they consume oxygen

T   E   R

and release CO_2. Similarly, the level of pollution in a river is expressed as a figure called the B.O.D. (biochemical oxygen demand). This shows how much oxygen is used by nitrobacteria in the oxidation of organic matter, and therefore is an indicator of the level of organic waste in the river.

LIGHTING

All plants need light, but aquaria cannot simply be placed by a window to solve this problem. Excess light is a major cause of algal growth in aquaria. The best way to manage the lighting of an aquarium is to put it in a position that gets absolutely no sunlight and rely entirely on artificial lighting. It is true that sunlight contributes to the health and luster of fishes, but ultraviolet light is unnecessary for bringing out the beauty of aquatic plants. In fact, aquatic plants raised indoors turn out much more beautifully than those raised outdoors.

There are several options for lighting, including mercury bulbs and halogen lamps, but flourescent lights are the best economically, esthetically, and practically. Many people mistakenly think that horticultural lamps are suitable for aquaria, but in fact the light that they give off only contains the three essential light waves for plants, making them suitable only for land plants like Saint Paulia. Another failing of this lamp is that its intensity is only about a third of conventional flourescent lamps (measured in luxes), making for a rather dark aquarium. Some prefer these because of the intense reds they produce, but personally I think that colors look weird under these lights.

Let's look at some concrete examples, though this may overlap the CO_2 section a bit. If, in a 60cm tank, we raise *Cryptocoryne* and *Anubias*, both broad-leaved, low photosynthesizing shade-loving plants, they will require one 20W high color-performance bulb and a dose of CO_2 with a large dispenser once a day. In the same tank, however, light-loving plants, such as the aforementioned red-stem types, will require three light bulbs and a drop of CO_2 added to the dispenser every five seconds in order to keep the plants looking good. When setting up the aquarium, it is important to try to place the light-loving plants directly under the bulbs, and reserve the spots that receive less direct light for the shade-loving plants.

Fluorescent bulbs begin to lose their intensity after about six months of use. An aquarium planted with both light-loving and shade-loving plants will change over time as a result of the wear on the lighting. At first, the light-loving plants thrive, and the *Cryptocoryne* and ferns stagnate. Then as the bulbs begin to fade, the ferns and the *Cryptocoryne* start to grow and eventually take over unless the bulbs are replaced.

L I G H T I N G &

The most commonly used type is a high color performance fluorescent bulb, which I think is best. Various types are available from large manufacturers, and there is little variation in light composition, intensity, or durability, so take your pick.

The amount of wattage necessary is related to the amount of CO_2 being added. If the light is very intense, but the plants don't receive a correspondingly larger amount of CO_2, then the light will harm them. If, on the other hand, the amount of CO_2 is increased without a corresponding increase in lighting, the plants will not photosynthesize well, and the CO_2 level will reach such a height as to harm the fishes and shrimp.

The balance between light and CO_2 depends on several factors, including water temperature and plant type. Plants can be divided into two major types here: light-loving plants (need sun) and shade-loving plants (grow in shade). Light-loving plants need both more light and more CO_2 than shade-loving plants. Such plants as *Anubias* and the ferns are considered easy to raise because they are shade-loving plants. They are highly adaptable to strong light enviroments and so are the most flexible plants.

Such plants as the Dutch plant and the needle leaf, which have narrow leaves and red stem coloration, are said to be difficult to raise, but this is because they require relatively high levels of both light and CO_2. They aren't flexible like shade-loving plants, but they are not different from other plants in any other respect.

SUBSTRATE

The substrate is the floor of sand in which the plants grow. Not a lot of research has been done on base sand, but its importance is obvious. Sea sand, such as Philippine sand and South Sea sand, is the most commonly used, but river sand is fairly popular. Some unusual sands are fired red clay, Fuji sand, volcanic sand, and ceramics.

Aquarium base sand must meet a few conditions. First and foremost it must not contain elements that adversely affect the water conditions. Most prominent here are coral and seashells, which will raise the pH and water hardness because of their high calcium content. Other materials that lower these two values can cause root rot, which in turn leads to algal growth. The pH of the sand itself should be neutral to slightly acidic (7-6.8), the ideal for most plant roots.

The granule size should be between 3 and 10mm. Larger granules will block root development, and sand made up of smaller ones will crush the roots. Base sand that is not permeable enough, like unfired clay, blocks the passage of important particles and prevents

that contain several different types of sand will have a longer lifetime, and arranging them in layers improves permeability. For example, for the bottom layer mix 5-10mm granule sand with 5-10mm size Fuji sand. Add in some sand base fertilizer, which can be bought in stores. Smooth out the layer at around 3cm. For the middle layer, repeat the procedure minus the fertilizer and with slightly finer sand and Fuji sand (5-7mm). Finally, for the top layer add 2cm of 5mm granule sand alone. Fuji sand, and other sand of volcanic origin, are too rough for the surface since it will damage young roots.

Fuji sand is mixed in to prevent lumping and hardening and to improve permeability. The roots of *Echinodorus* and *Cryptocoryne* are surprisingly thick, and the spaces between regular sand are just too tight for them. If Fuji sand is unavailable, it is best to mix sands of different granule sizes. It is safe to use pre-mixed sand sold in stores when the tank depth is under 45cm.

Fertilizer should be added only to the bottom layer so it seeps into the water slowly enough to avoid algal

B A S E   S A N D

the flow of oxygen that the roots need. Sand that isn't smooth will damage roots during planting.

Any base sand that meets these conditions is safe to use in an aquarium, but glass beads, colored ceramics, and other unnatural materials are not recommended for esthetic reasons.

Next, let's consider what types of substrate different plants want to put down roots into. There are three broad groups of aquatic plants classified by root types. First are the plants that don't need sand, but instead attach their roots to rocks or driftwood, such as *Anubias, Microsorium*, and *Bolbitis*. Next are the plants with large root stocks, like *Aponogeton* and *Nymphaea*, and the long-stemmed plants, like *Hygrophila* and *Rotala*, that have shallow roots. Last are the deep-root plants like *Cryptocoryne* and *Echinodorus*.

These plants all have corresponding substrate needs which must be met. If the substrate is not deep enough for the last type, for example, the roots will become entangled and the plants, which obtain most of their nutrients and oxygen through their roots, will be asphyxiated. *Echinodorus tenellus* and *E. grisebachii*, both of which have long rhizome runners, need at least a 6cm deep substrate.

When the aquarium contains all three root types, as it often does, it is necessary to create a substrate that will accommodate the deep-rooted plants. Substrates

growths of various types. When filling the tank, the water should be poured gently into a plate or bowl placed on the sand to avoid churning up the fertilizer.

AQUATIC PLANT FERTILIZER

No material for raising plants is available in as many brands and names as fertilizer. The two primary types are solid fertilizer, which is mixed in with the sand, and liquid fertilizer, which is added periodically to the water.

The first kind is useful when planting deep-rooted plants, as we saw earlier, but they do have a major disadvantage. If algae is becoming a problem and too much fertilizer is the suspected reason, it is impossible to dig up the bottom layer and remove it. Therefore, it is better to err on the side of caution when adding base sand fertilizer. But this fertilizer has a powerful effect on plants that can be clearly seen, since it is absorbed by the roots.

Liquid fertilizer, however, is absorbed by the leaves, and is therefore not going to have a dramatic effect on the plants' condition. On the other hand, the amount administered is much easier to control by simply changing the water. Most aquarists use liquid fertilizers, but I prefer the effectiveness of substrate fertilizer.

One way to avoid solid fertilizer trouble is to watch the water closely for clouding when initially filling the tank. Then change the water repeatedly until it clears up.

F E R T I L I Z E R &

The fertilizer will eventually settle into the sand and stop floating up into the water.

Almost everyone uses liquid fertilizers but almost no one uses them well. The instructions rarely take into account the amount or type of plant. Fish foods rarely tell how much to add to such and such a size aquarium, because it is easy to figure out how much by watching the fishes. If they haven't eaten everything, no one would add more. However, plants aren't as easy to figure out. Unfortunately, when plants are looking bad, a lot of people seem to assume that they need more nutrition and add more fertilizer. This just winds up killing the plants most of the time.

Plant health can be determined by noting the pH levels, whether the leaves are shiny, if new buds are appearing, if algae is growing on the plants, and other such simple observations. The amount of fertilizer shouldn't be changed until the various aspects I have discussed are all checked out. One exception is whitening of leaves and buds. This is a clear sign of malnutrition.

DAILY CARE/CHANGING THE WATER

Changing the aquarium water is the most laborious job of the aquarist, but putting it off leads to algal growth and sick fishes. It is impossible to say exactly how much and how often, but as a general rule the water should be changed at least two or three times a month. Tap water is rich in CO_2 and important substances and should be fine.

Sometimes people complain that their fishes died from changing the water. This is almost always a case where the water hadn't been changed in a long time. The fishes were affected by either pH shock (the old water must have become acidic) or a sudden drop in the amount of filter bacteria (especially if the filter was cleaned at the same time, always a bad idea), which led to sudden acidification. The trick is simply to change the water gradually, gently, and often.

SUMMER AND WINTER CARE

Plants should be watched closely in hot summer weather, even when we are feeling lazy, since they are more sensitive to heat than we are. The aquarium should be kept in a continually air-conditioned room near the A/C. Otherwise, an aquarium cooler is recommended. The ideal temperature for most aquatic plants is around 28°C, and they can withstand temperatures of up to 31° or 32° for short periods. Water is generally two degrees cooler than the room temperature, so it should be set at 30°C. Of course, the lighting has to be taken into account as well. A fan directed at the aquarium will lower the temperature a few degrees. Some aquarists float bags of ice in the aquarium as a temporary measure.

A more troublesome but effective way to lower the temperature is to change 70-80% of the water. Chlorine is less soluble in warm summer water, so even large water changes won't lead to chlorine poisoning. Frequent water changes will promote growth during the regularly stagnate summer months. The lack of growth during the summer is natural but is often mistakenly handled by adding more fertilizer.

A D M I N I S T R A T I O N

Aquatic plants are at their best in winter. There is little special treatment to worry about, but some sort of heater is necessary unless there is continuous climate control. A simple heater and thermostat system is easily set up, but the heater should have a lower electrical capacity than the thermostat. For example, if the thermostat's capacity is 300W, the heater should have a limit of around 250W. Thermostats often break as a result of strain, using more electricity than their capacity, so there should be a safety factor.

Most heaters do not affect the bottom of the aquarium enough, and roots can be damaged. This is especially a problem with aquaria that are kept in cold areas so that the thermostat is always on. One way to prevent heat loss through the bottom is to place styrofoam underneath and around the lower half of the sides of the aquarium. Bottom heaters, another option, should have their own thermostats to prevent overheating the roots.

The chlorine content of cold water is high, so water changes should be less frequent in winter. When the water is heated in a boiler, tiny bubbles of chlorine are formed which can get caught in the gills of fishes and do them great harm. Water should be changed a little at a time and aerated with an air stone or by pouring it from bucket to bucket in order to dispel some of the chlorine gas.

THE CAUSES OF OUTBREAKS OF ALGAE

The greatest obstruction to beautiful aquatic plants is algal growth. It is also the number-one cause of stress among aquarists. There are many species that are difficult to eradicate. Some of the most common are brown algae, string algae (keijoo-sou), beard algae (higejou-sou), norijou-soo, and aomidori. The causes of algal outbreaks are numerous, so it is always difficult to say why one has occurred.

The brown algae appears when the aquarium is young, is brown in color, and covers everything from walls to driftwood to leaves like a thin curtain. It is easily dealt with by adding a natural enemy, the best of which is *Otocinclus*. *Plecos* also eat it, but they may damage the leaves as well. The algae eater (*Gyrinocheilus aymonieri*) and the Siamese flying fox (*Crossocheilus siamensis*) also eat brown algae, but grow too large for a small tank or crowded layout.

The string algae appears as long, thin strings attached to driftwood, rocks, filter tubes, and old leaves. It may be green, gray or black, but is usually green in well-lit places. Outbreaks can be caused by infrequent water changes (high nitrate level) or too strong lighting (CO_2

Aomidoro grows around the surfaces of plants, entangling in the dense growth of *Riccia* or willow moss and becoming difficult to remove. It thrives in the same conditions as aquarium plants, so it is not easily taken care of with water changes. But many shrimp, otamajackshi, black mollies, dwarf cichlids, and other fishes feed on it so it is relatively easy to handle.

Many other algae exist, and most outbreaks are a result of excess nitrates from too many fishes and infrequent water changes, dirty filters, or CO_2/light imbalances. They can be largely prevented by cultivating the following good habits.

*Don't put fishes into an aquarium right away. Wait rather for the plants' roots to take hold and new buds to appear, than add the fishes a few at a time.

*Change the water immediately if it appears that substrate fertilizer is seeping into the water.

*Use a large filter box, and at the beginning use three parts activated charcoal to one part bacteria filtration. Bacteria culture on a hard surface is best.

*In the early stages, there are not enough bacteria and the pH is high, so lower it with CO_2 doses. Do not use

F O R E I G N   E N

deficiency). This nuisance can be prevented by keeping the yamato numa-ebi shrimp and bee shrimp in the aquarium from the start.

Beard algae is longer and thicker than string algae, but grows as a result of the same imbalances. It appears in relatively older tanks, growing on hard leaves like that of *Anubias* and *Kurinam*. Yamato numa-ebi won't eat it once it grows to a large size, so the shrimp should be kept in the tank from the beginning as a preventive measure. It doesn't grow profusely, but it is very unattractive. When changing water, it can be scraped off with your fingernails or sucked up with a vacuum. The red scat will clean an infested tank, but certain preparations need to be made for it. The pH level should be pushed up to around 7.5 or higher by stopping CO_2 doses and, if necessary, adding potassium carbonate. Of course, the specimen must be one that has been acclimated to fresh water.

Nori jou algae is a bright green, mold-like algae that grows on the bottom sand and leaves. It produces a strong, moldy odor. It will break out in tanks with new filters and alkaline water, or as a result of too much light. Vacuuming is only a temporary measure because it grows back very quickly. A good quality filter is the best measure, and special herbicides or malachite green can also wipe out nori.

chemicals to lower it.

*Keep the temperature low during the early stages of the aquarium, around 22-23°C. The ideal temperature for aquatic plants is 24-25°C.

*Don't use liquid fertilizers soon after planting. Wait until roots have taken and new growth appears.

*Nitrobacteria need time to develop, so a new filter box relies on activated charcoal. During this early time, water changes should be made at least once a week.

*Use a lot of long-stemmed plants in the background at first. They will absorb excess nutrients and, as they grow, serve to regulate the amount of light.

*Keep some *Otocinclus* and yamato numa-ebi shrimp in the aquarium from the start to prevent algal growth.

PREVENTION AND ERADICATION OF SNAILS AND LEECHES

The beautiful red ramshorn snail has enjoyed some deserved popularity in the past. It doesn't take over the aquarium. But inferior snails suddenly appear out of nowhere and occupy every inch. It is extremely difficult to remove the eggs from plants before they are transplanted into the tank, and vacuuming them during water changes never completely wipes them out.

The dwarf cichlids are the best anti-snail weapon. Also good are *Anabas*, the South American puffer, and the dwarf frog (shime-gaeru). Even these natural enemies won't feed on the snails if they aren't hungry or have other food to eat, so it's a good idea to starve them for a while before putting them in.

Leeches, hydra, and other coelenterates may infest aquaria as well, and they are also fed on by the dwarf shime-gaeru, so this animal ranks highly with the yamato numa-ebi shrimp for pest control.

TRIMMING AQUATIC PLANTS

When plants are healthy and flourishing, they eventually fill the tank and make it look like an unkempt lawn. They need to be periodically trimmed and thinned.

Long-stemmed plants should be trimmed to a proper size with an eye on the balance of the entire layout. The scissors should be as long and sharp as possible. Two or three new leaves will grow from each cut, so the plants may become top-heavy with growth after too much trimming, and the stems will break easily. When this starts to happen, trim the plants less often and higher up on the stem.

When plants that grow from runners, like *E. tenellus,*

become too big or old. *Microsorium* develops black spores under its leaves for reproduction. The ugly spores and secondary rhizomes should be removed carefully so as not to damage the primary rhizome.

Plants with large root stocks, such as water lilies and *Aponogeton*, have growing seasons and dormant seasons, so just when they seem to be growing well, growth will suddenly stop and leaves start to die in such numbers that they can ruin the water quality and clog the filter. When the dormant season begins, immediately begin removing dead leaves before they become a problem.

Finally, some water lilies (lotus, for example) have leaves that float on the surface. Not only do these block the aquarist's top view, but they also block light from reaching the plants below. It's safer to cut them before they affect any other plants.

AQUATIC PLANT DISEASES

Since aquatic plants live in a closed and clean enviroment, a smaller number of diseases affect them than land plants. I have seen a few diseases, such as

E   M   Y   &   S   I   C   K

Glossostigma, Vallisneria, and *Sagittaria,* become too thick, their roots will suffocate unless they are trimmed. *Sagittaria* and *Vallisneria* don't grow over themselves no matter how thick they get, so simply removing dead leaves from time to time is sufficient. *E. tenellus* and *Glossostigma* are small plants, however, and when they become dense the leaves will pile up five or six deep and the lower ones will become completely asphyxiated. These grow along the walls, so carefully cut and remove the runner around 7cm from the wall to prevent overgrowth.

Willow moss and ferns that are attached to rocks and driftwood should be trimmed like hair: when they get too long. Once willow moss has taken to the surface, it can be thinned pretty roughly without fear of it coming loose, but trimming neatly with scissors is best.

Anubias never grows to the point where it dominates the layout. Leaves that are too large, old-looking, ragged from being fed on, or algae-covered should be removed right away. The genus *Anubias* is especially susceptible to algal infestation, so leaves should be removed as soon as any unwanted life form shows up on them. New leaves will grow in.

Ferns such as *Microsorium* and *Bolbitis* grow surprisingly quickly and will soon throw off the balance of the layout. Leaves should be removed once they

when blackish, nearly transparent wrinkles spread rapidly through some *Microsorium*, but not so many. The most common seems to be *Cryptocoryne* disease, where its leaves and stems crumple up instantly. But this is not a disease at all, but rather a shock reaction to sudden changes in the water chemistry, such as a drastic pH drop from adding too much CO_2, or a sudden increase in light intensity from a bulb change. However, if measures are taken its recovery is almost as fast.

If the aquarium's upkeep is good, aquatic plants almost never get sick. Many plants are sensitive to fish medicines, even those whose labels say they are safe. Generally, an unhealthy enviroment is caused by too many fishes in the aquarium, a dirty filter, acidification of the water from high nitrate levels, or too much leftover food piling up. Regular water changes, especially in warm weather, a large filter box, a small number of fishes, and cleaning up after feedings add up to healthy and beautiful plants. If, by a stroke of bad luck, some disease does afflict the plants, quickly transplant the unaffected plants to another tank and start over.

EPILOGUE

Humans, the newcomers on this four billion-year-old planet, now have the power to destroy nature. The once-clear water is muddied, and the once-green land is losing its color. In trying to make their lives rich, people have made us all incredibly poorer from the destruction of nature. Only desolate hearts can grow in desolate surroundings. We have to remember that we either live in nature or not at all.

Through building and maintaining beautiful natural aquaria, people relearn the intricate connections between forms of life: plants, fishes, microorganisms, and humans. Riches and beauty come from harmony, from balance. Aquaria are great teachers of this truth.

Takashi Amano January 6, 1992

TAKASHI'S WONDERFUL STORY

 When I first met Takashi Amano I was a teacher in his junior high school. The Yoroi Wetlands, the biggest wetlands in Niigata Prefecture, were nearby, full of aquatic plants, freshwater fishes, and waterfowl. It was famous for the several species of dragonflies that were native to it. The wetlands were going to be drained, though, so I started a biology club and led the kids on expeditions to research the aquatic life there. Takashi joined it. It was a wonderful group, some of whom won national awards, and Takashi was hard at work studying the chosen-buna.

 He was a creative and sensitive high school student, a National Meet cyclist, a painter of watercolors, and the first to start a movement in Niigata to protect the local enviroment. As he grew older, he toured the country as an A-class cyclist and devoted his remaining energy to his passion, tropical fishes, building the knowledge base that would lead to the opening of his own shop.

 One day he came to me and said he was going to concentrate on aquatic plants. I was ignorant of tropical fishes in those days and didn't understand what he meant. He explained that in Germany it was becoming popular to build miniature ecosystems with plants and raise fishes in them. He was excited, but worried that it wouldn't provide a living. We talked about the difficulties of creating the correct conditions. I was amazed by how quickly he mastered the necessary knowledge, and how beautifully his aquariums turned out.

 I think Takashi has been the organizer of a revolution against the old, rigid concept of aquaria, which were just glass boxes for viewing fishes. He has made the plants the stars, and raised the work of aquarists to an art form.

 Now Takashi and I are more like brothers than like a teacher and a student. I am extremely happy to see his work published, and I hope he continues to explore new genres.

Dr. Nagashima, Professor, Niigata Seiryo Women's Junior College

ABOUT THE AUTHOR

Takashi Amano (Born July 18, 1954)

Mr. Amano became interested in aquatic plants and animals at an early age and won the prefecture prize for scientific research for his Korean paradise fish studies in junior high school. He began studying and experimenting with the relationships between fishes and plants at this time. In 1976, he began publishing photographs and essays on tropical fishes and plants from his travels in Africa, Asia, and Japan's southern islands.

He started building and photographing plant aquaria in 1972. He entered his first photo contest, the JPS '91, in 1991 with "Chameleon Diary" winning top honors and "Leading Ladies in Shade" selected for exhibition. His "Yamor" won a silver medal at the Fuji Film Nature Photo Contest in the same year. He has also won several honors at the prefectural and city levels in Niigata.

Mr. Amano was a professional cyclist from 1974 to 1990, but at present he devotes his energy to running Aqua-design Amano, a specialty store and maker of plant aquarium products.

PROFILE

野 尚（あまの　たかし）

和29年（1954年）7月18日生まれ。

少の頃より水棲の動植物に興味を持ち、中
時代の研究発表会で「チョウセンブナの研
」が県の優秀賞を受賞。また、その頃から熱
魚に興味を持ち、動植物の共存関係を念頭
、水草と魚を共存させた飼育を始める。昭
51年（1976年）から、ケニア、タンザニア、南
エメン、エチオピア、エジプト、ウガンダ、イン
、さらに南西諸島の島々を数回にわたって
れ、熱帯における魚や水草の生態写真、エッ
イを専門誌に発表する。

草のレイアウトは、昭和47年（1972年）頃から
り始め、同時に水槽の写真撮影も手掛ける。
成3年（1991年）には、写真コンテストに初め
出品し、'91JPS展で「カメレオンダイアリ
」が優秀賞、「木かげの主役たち」が入選。ま
'91フジフィルム・ネイチャーフォトコンテスト
「ヤモリ」が銀賞を受賞。この他、県展・新潟
写真家協会展入選等多数の受賞がある。
和49年（1974年）～平成2年（1990年）まで16
間、自転車のプロ選手として活躍していたが、
在は水草栽培関連商品メーカー兼専門ショ
プ「アクアデザイン　アマノ」を主宰している。

I want to extend my deepest appreciation for the help given to me by Professor Kawanabe of Kyoto University, Dr. Nagashima of Niigata Seiryo Women's Junior College, and Keiji Ishizu of Marine Planning, who knocked himself out helping to bring this book to publication. I thank all of you.
Takashi Amano January 6, 1992

Useful Conversions and Equivalents

Water Weight

1. A gallon of water weighs:
Imperial		USA	
10 lb	4.5 kg	8.3 lb	3.8 kg

2. A liter of water weighs 1 kg or 2.2 lb.

3. A pint of water weighs:
Imperial		USA	
1.25 lb	0.57 kg	1.04 lb	0.47 kg

4. 1 cubic foot of salt water = 64 lb
   1 cubic foot of fresh water = 62.43 lb

Gallon Equivalents

1 Imp. gallon = 1.2 US gallons = 4.55 liters

1 US gallon = 0.833 Imp. gallons = 3.78 liters

1 Liter = 0.264 US gallons = 0.22 Imp gallons

1 Imp. gallon = 277 in^3 = 4,542 cm^3

1 US gallon = 231 in^3 = 3,685 cm^3

Liter Equivalents

1 Liter = 1,000 cm^3 = 61 in^3
      = 1 Kilogram
      = 1.76 Imp pints = 2.11 US
      Pints

Weight

1 Kilogram = 1,000 grams = 2.2 lb = 35.2 oz
1 Pound = 0.45 kg = 454 grams
1 Ounce = 28.35 grams
1 Hundredweight = 112 lb = 50.8 kg

Measurements

Length x Width = Surface area

1 inch = 2.54 centimeters

1 cm = 0.39 in

12 inch = 30.48 cm = 0.3048 meters

1 m = 39.37 in = 3.28 ft

1 Tablespoon = 3 teaspoons = 1/2 fluid oz

1 Teaspoon = 1/6 fluid oz = 1.3 fluid drams

1 Pint = 16 fl oz = 128 fl drams

1 Fl.dram = 3.7 mils or cc

Temperature

° Celsius x 1.8 + 32 = ° Fahrenheit

° Fahrenheit - 32 x 0.556 = ° Celsius

Each 1° Celsius change in temperature = 1.8
  ° Fahrenheit
(e.g. If the temperature of water is raised 3°
C, this will add 5.4 ° to the Fahrenheit
temperature.)

Electricity

Power (Watts) = Current (Amps) x Voltage

Amps = Watts divided by Volts